From Grief to Grind

THE JOURNEY OF DENIAL, ACCEPTANCE, AND PURPOSE

Compiled by Andrea A. Moore

KylaNicole (KN) Publishing

Copyright © 2018 by Andrea Moore

All rights reserved. No part of this publication may be reproduced, distributed or transmitted in any form or by any means, without prior written permission.

Andrea Moore/KylaNicole Publishing
Glendora Drive
Powder Springs, GA 30127
www.KylaNicole.org

Book Layout © 2016 BookDesignTemplates.com

From Grief to Grind/ Andrea A. Moore -- 1st ed.
ISBN 978-0-692-16610-9

Dedication

From Grief to Grind is dedicated in memory of my grandmother Mary R. Ruffin, my grandfather Charlie Foster, and Yolanda Foster. Although they are not here in the flesh I know they are smiling ear to ear. I can hear my grandfather telling me to keep God first, my grandmother saying You did it, and my cousin saying Say it cuz. Thank you God for giving me the moments I had with them.

Acknowledgements

First and foremost all praises go to the creator. I thank him for allowing me to be a vessel. To the 8 amazing women telling their story. I am honored that we meet, cried on the phone, laughed, and are able to speak on our real truth. We are always going to be connected and you will always be my sisters.

Tyrone Moore-Thank you for always being supportive. Never doubting the vision that God has given me. I would not be the woman I am if it hadn't been for the love, friendship, and marriage that we have.

Mom (Bettye Ruffin Jackson)-As a little girl I remember you encouraging me to enjoy life. As I've gotten older those are the words that stick with me. During this Grief journey we have cried, kicked, and scream. I am grateful for that. You've never questioned my vision and your support is much appreciated. Thank you mom for everything.

Lakshmia Ferba-Business Bestie oh how I love you. You've seen me at my worse and at my best. Thank you for being the best business partner, friend, and truth teller. We sisters for real.

Quashana Foster-My spiritual advisor, cousin, friend, and child of God. Oh man the talks and the tears that we've shared I am in awe of both of our growth. Thank you a million times for giving me the word and heartfelt love during this project.

Dad (Jesse C. Foster)-Deacon Foster you are truly appreciated. You listen to me and give me words of wisdom and prayer. I know even when I am not joking you are praying for me. I thank the creator for you every day.

Editor (Jarius)-I use to wonder how people connect. Then I wondered why people connected. Then when I started to really understand my journey then I said. "I am so thankful for being connected to an amazing person. Jarius every day I appreciate you. Not only as an intuitive editor but as a friend. Thank you for being apart of this project.

KN Publishing-Who knew that one phone conversation would lead to this. Thank you KN Publishing for being a part of this project. You did an amazing job. I don't know if I could've done this project without you.

My Canvas Beauty and Photography-What an amazing team. Thank you so much for capturing our essence.

Author Acknowledgement

Sherri Leopold- Words cannot express how I am so honored to have you in this book. You are one of my inspirations. Thank you so much Sherri.

Nicole Redmond-To watch you evolve and go through grief during this project shows me that we are forever tied. Thank you so much for being a part of this moment.

Hope Marsh-From the moment we spoke. I knew that we are kindred souls. To have you apart of this movement is an honor. Thank you so much.

Dorsetta Clark-Davis-Your story and your journey has me in tears. To watch you daily grow close to the God is a sight to see. Thank you for being so candid about your journey.

Myesha Collins-When you said that you were willing to be in this project who knew what you would
go through during all of this. Thank you for being transparent and smiling all the way through.

Phoenix J-Watching you grow through what you went through has been an honor but to really hear you is
a sound unheard of. Thank you so much for being a part of this project.

Kyla Nicole-Kyla you an amazing women of purpose and one who has made an impact on this world. Thank you for being Kyla and sharing your story. I appreciate you more then you know.

D'Niesha Shields-To be so young and ready to be so honest tells me that it is your time to build within to help others. I am so proud of you and all that your doing. Thank you for sharing your story.

Table of Content

Chapter One:
The Long and Winding Road of Indestructibility
By: Hope Marsh

Chapter Two:
The Triumph of the Unshakable Grief
By: KylaNicole

Chapter Three:
Death of Me
By: Nicole Redmond

Chapter Four:
The Spirit Within-Love and Lust
By: Phoenix J'Mari

Chapter Five:
My Pride and Joy is Now Gone
By: Dorsetta Clark-Davis

Chapter Six:
Release Grief-Obtain Love
By: Myesha Collins

Chapter Seven:
Is There a Rainbow at the End of the storm?
By: Sherri Leopold

Chapter Eight:
Redeemed
By: D'Niesha Johnson-Shields

Note to Reader

Dear reader,

I want to thank you for purchasing this book. The inspiration from this book comes from the loss of my sister. Dealing with grief I then found out that since age 8 I have not grieved. I witnessed my parents divorced, by age 27 I lost moments in life because I was living for someone else, lost myself, lost a home, relationships, and unfortunately so much more. I never dealt with grief I just went on like nothing happened.

I watched my sister and mom in love fight for their life it was hard for me to breath. Witnessing others lose themselves, fight anxiety, unforgiven many, walk around like everything is okay, and be at an emotional standstill. It hurt hell to watch.

We didn't mourn and we have to. Why? We weren't taught to or we just don't know how. At some point it was time to deal. The hurt happened and now it is time to walk real close and face head on.

I know you're ready to hear these powerful women.

Thanks again!

We appreciate you,

Andrea A. Moore & Co-authors

CHAPTER ONE

The Long and Winding Road of Indestructibility

Call me Ishmael. Some years ago—never mind how long precisely—having little or no money in

Part I

    Ever since high school, I'd been in search for my one true love: just a nice guy who'd love me. Once discovered, I'd go above and beyond. No distance too far, no neighborhood too questionable. Growing up *urban-adjacent*, I'd no access to a car, so I'd walk, catch the bus, or even take a cab-which they almost never offered to pay for). This continued on, well into young adulthood. I dated guys without cars, jobs; and, even those who thought I was a "good woman" but just weren't quite ready to settle down. I figured, I didn't want to "kick a brother while he was down", so I put up with their emotional ambivalence, low ambition, and their lack of resources.

    I wasn't sure where I picked up this desperation for a man, as it was the complete opposite of the messaging I'd received from my mother. A Caribbean immigrant, who came to the US in the early 70's, she stressed the value of hard work, self-sufficiency, and most of all, not to depend on a man for anything. Thus, I always knew from an early age, perhaps around 6, that I never wanted children. Me not liking children wasn't a motivator, but more so, how irresponsibly the adults involved in creating the children, behaved, and how quickly people disappear, and someone was left alone to be a parent. Early in my Navy career, when I was 20, I'd made the tough decision to terminate a pregnancy. However; to understand my story, I suppose I should start from the beginning. Not with myself, but with my mother.

    After much coaxing from her grandmother, who'd believed that a young woman deserved a better life than taking care of some old lady, my mother left the small Caribbean island of Barbados for the United States in 1973. She was already well into her 20's, which by most accounts is considered "late" as most people come over during childhood, usually at the accompaniment of an elder. Upon her arrival, my mother wound up living in Baltimore with her Uncle and his wife, who themselves had left the island some years earlier. Almost immediately, Mum attained a job cleaning houses; a job to which another fellow islander referred her. As if an arduous commute by bus, and low wages weren't enough, she also endured constant bigotry: being accused of stealing silverware, having to bring her own cups to drink from (as they didn't want her using theirs), and being relegated to "learn the language", even though she spoke English. But she needed the money, so she endured.

Eventually Mum had moved out of her uncle's house and settled in the Park Heights section of West Baltimore. Also, by this time, she'd attained her Geriatric Nursing Assistant (GNA) certificate and had begun work at a nursing home. This is where she met my father. Her co-worker at the time, who also happened to be my fathers' cousin, introduced them after he' repeatedly inquired about my mother. My mother still hadn't gotten a car by this time, so initially, she'd get a ride to the bus stop. Eventually, my father started taking her the rest of the way home. After a quick courtship, they became a couple.

By Moms' account, my father was a nice man. Unfortunately, she said, he just didn't have much of a backbone with it came to his own father. Apparently, his father, who was a retired railroad worker in some capacity, had shares in the company. As such, he'd accumulated a modest, but substantial nest egg for himself. Every chance his father got, Mom said, he'd dangle the money in his children's faces, threatening to cut them out of the will for some, 'thing', or "another" of which he disapproved. Now, my father had a brother. He was very strong willed, and frequently told his father where he could shove the money. Let's just say, it wasn't in a box under the mattress. But my father, just didn't have the gumption to do so. When Mum questioned his inability to stand up for himself, my father simply shrugged, saying "oh he's an old man, he's got nobody, and I don't want to be another person who turns his back on him." In addition to being miserly, my fraternal grandfather was also a cheat, and frequently swindled people out of their money, with some scheme or another. His ways caught up to him eventually, in that he cheated an old Haitian woman out of some money. As the story goes, the woman put a "root" (pronounced *ruht*) on him, and threatened that the same deceitful hand he used to steal from her, will be the same hand that shrivels up like a raisin in a weeks' time. Now, the hand could have shriveled up for a number of reasons: old age, too long of a time in the bath, an allergic reaction. Or even on account of the psychosomatic effects of a guilty conscience. A week later, though, as predicted, he developed said condition. Because of this, he was convinced that all Caribbean women were capable of such, and forbade my father from continuing his relationship with my mother. He'd already disapproved of my fathers' relationship with my mother from the start, and his negative experience with the Haitian woman only made his contempt for my mother, even worse.

Yet, my father continued seeing my mother. It was no surprise when I came along. Naturally, she shared the news with my father. I never asked my Mum how my father took the news, and at this time, I'm afraid to. So we'll leave it there for now. But sadly, and unbeknownst to her, my father had been seeing another woman, and she too, was pregnant, and, with a little girl. However; it was my mother's pregnancy that elicited the visceral reaction from my grandfather--not the fact that he'd had 2 women pregnant at the same time, which was pretty irresponsible, even for those times (I was born in 1975), but that I was coming into the world. He'd convinced my father that the child wasn't his, as my mother was a foreigner, without a green card, and was probably just looking for a sponsor. Never mind that my mother had been working literally the second she set foot in this country, and had already attained her green card upon arrival. Somehow, his father convinced him otherwise. Up until I began to walk, Mum said, my father would make half-hearted attempts to engage with us. He still lived at home, and appeared to be "sneaking around" to see my mother. Perhaps Mum didn't want to feel like some dirty little secret. Perhaps she told him to stand up for us, or don't come back. Whatever the conversation, he slowly stopped coming around, and then, not at all.

Given that my father had chosen not support the family in any way, things were tight financially. Thank God for her fellow Caribbean immigrant friends, who stepped in when and where they could: either to baby sit, to comb my hair, to lend money, to buy food. Despite her best efforts though, Mum eventually had to apply for food stamps. Back then, it was colorful currency, bearing the words "Food Coupon" on the front; under the auspices of the Department of Agriculture. Even for what seemed a minute and short-term subsidy, Mum reported being questioned during the initial application process, as to whether or not she had mice, roaches, or other vermin running rampant in the home, as if this were a sort of poverty 'barometer', by which to judge if we were "poor enough" and therefore deserving of services. Though we weren't 'dirt poor', by any means, we weren't living high on the hog. Hand-me-downs and Goodwill shopping trips were aplenty, as was walking and/or taking the bus virtually everywhere. There was also the occasional interruption of utilities, such as gas & electric and telephone, as well as the periodic late rent reminder, plastered on the door. Today, shopping at the Goodwill is considered trendy; back then, it just meant you were poor.

Mum eventually attained another job at a better nursing home, where she'd worked the 3rd shift. Prior to my being taken to the neighbor's house for the night, I'd watched as Mum proudly put on her uniform, always ironed to perfection. She would wipe her nursing shoes with a sponge, before applying the white shoe polish. She had an awesome afro, kept her nails polished and always wore perfume. If I was good, she would motion for me to hold out my wrist, so she could spray it with the fragrance. It didn't matter that she was going to spend the next 8 hours changing the soiled sheets and diapers of the elderly. Mum had a strong work ethic. She had zero tolerance for idleness. She especially didn't care for whistling, as she'd argued that if a person has time to whistle, they have time to do something productive. Sleeping in on Saturday mornings was out of the question: there were floors to be swept, dishes to wash, toys to put away, and errands to run. It was drummed into my head that if I wanted to succeed, I'd need to work hard. I would listen in awe when she would share stories of her growing up in Barbados: waking up at 5am to tend to the pigs and chickens before school, the scar on her ankle she'd gotten from tending to said pigs and chickens, and dumping water on the heads of childhood bullies.

Given her industriousness, Mum eventually gained her socio-economic footing. She transitioned off food stamps and settled into single motherhood. Even still, as a young child, I couldn't articulate what a "single mother" was, or, that there was anything wrong with it. I thought it was normal. I simply saw it as having my mother all to myself. That is, until I got to school.

"Where's your father", the children asked, to which I'd innocently replied, "I don't have one". They'd all laughed incredulously, and would retort: "that's dumb, everyone has a daddy. "Well not me", I'd said, rather defiantly. In my mind, it was really that simple: *"I just didn't have one"*. Who knew that a person, I had never even met, would continue to have such a profound impact on my life? My childhood taught me 2 things: I would never have children, lest I risk raising them alone; if I wanted to have a better life, I would have to work hard, and not be foolish enough to believe any man could be depended upon to help me. I've always worked. Industriousness, as passed down from my mother, is a virtue by which I define myself. You might call me a lot of things, but lazy will never be one of them. Even throughout high school, I had a job; I worked in fast food, and eventually, in retail. I paid for my own senior portraits, my prom, and my cap & gown. After graduation, I wanted out of Baltimore on the first thing smoking. College was out of the question. There simply was no money for it, and quite frankly, at that time, I didn't want to go, anyway.

I've always functioned at a baseline melancholy my whole life. Maybe because I was an only child with way too much time on my hands. I was extremely sensitive, almost always anxious, and worrying about something. Anything. Needless to say, I was grossly ill-equipped to do the self-work necessary to heal properly. Yet, I was determined to leave my brokenness behind. So at 19, I joined the Navy.

Part II

November 9, 1994. Recruit Training Command, Great Lakes, Illinois.

As soon as I stepped off that bus from Midway Airport, I realized I was in for a "world of hurt" – a phrase with which I'd become uncomfortably familiar. Company commanders swarmed us, from all over the base it seemed, yelling in our ears and in our faces. Telling us our asses belonged to them now. And for the next 8 weeks, they were right. Girls from all 4 corners of the United States became *Company 061, Division 2*. Initially, we were a large company (we started off with 90 women) and we had 2 Company commanders: Steffee and Chambers. I had no idea what their first names were, and no one dared ask. For the next 8 weeks, we woke up at ungodly hours of the morning for exercise, uniform inspections, and classes on Naval customs and history. And if by chance you couldn't recall said custom or history, you were punished with exercise – the *world of hurt* I'd mentioned before. Also, we were almost never allowed to talk. Anywhere. This turned out to be my albatross. For this infraction, I was often punished with push-ups, sit-ups, or straight 100 jumping jacks. Oh, and one mustn't forget the assembly-line style of administering for vaccinations and other medical procedures. The Navy does not nurture; it sustains you just enough to keep the equipment running. It seemed I subconsciously sought out personification of an absentee father, and a tapped out single mother.

Given my melancholic temperament, it is a wonder I made it out of boot camp, but I did. While we didn't get a direct choice for our next duty station, we could pick whether or not we wanted East or West Coast, or overseas. I picked West Coast. By February 1995, I arrived at my first duty station, Naval Air Facility, El Centro, California, about 2 hours east of San Diego. The terrain was flat; summers were extremely hot and dry, and the cooler months brought dust storms. Given that I'd initially enlisted in the Navy *undesignated*, or, without an assigned rate/specialty, I was assigned to where the need was greatest: the base recycling and hazardous material center. It was a hard and dirty job. But I'd discovered there was a sort of freedom in arduousness, so eventually, I'd come to enjoy it. Additionally, I learned to drive manual transmission on a 2 ton truck, operate a cardboard bailer, and to this day, I still recycle.

Given that I was new to the Navy, and to the base, I was not at all interested in dating. I didn't have a lot of civilian clothes and my hair hadn't quite grown back from the butchering of a haircut I'd gotten in boot camp, so didn't even feel that attractive, anyway. And so it went, for a few months. I'd fallen into a comfortable routine of work, socializing, and eating in the dining hall. Now, this wasn't to say I didn't notice the men around the base. One such guy in particular, we'll call him Dude. He was viscerally attractive, in great shape, and overall way better looking than me. So I'd managed to steer clear. Given my style of dress, and propensity to isolate, I'd earned the reputation of being a bit of a homely weirdo. But one afternoon in particular, a few of us were all in the dining hall, and Dude starting talking with me.

I was flattered that he would even look at me, much less talk to me. Perhaps he was bored. Perhaps he'd sensed I had low self-esteem, and would be easy prey. Who knows? Now I don't say the last part to paint myself as a victim, but to acknowledge my complicity in eventually, breaking my own heart. After a mere few weeks of mediocre conversation, Dude became a part of my routine, and so began a sexual affair, shrouded in secrecy and ambiguity. We didn't go out. He didn't buy me things. He did nothing, actually. But sexually, that man took me places I'd never been. Up until then, I'd never experienced an orgasm. I'd become an addict of sorts, chasing pleasure from him, however short-lived. Further, holding true to the old adage of the drunken sailor, I'd quietly developed a drinking problem, and regularly drank with the sole purpose of being drunk. Sometimes, our hook-ups were sober. Other times, not so much. This was the case with condoms; sometimes we'd use them, and other times, we take our chances with the pull out method. Naturally, these types of encounters don't last long, and we eventually burned out like a supernova. Following said burn out, irresponsible hedonism eventually came to collect her debt. After a missed period, one of the shore patrolmen on the base took pity on me, and purchased the pregnancy test for me from the Exchange (the on-base version of Walmart), because I'd been too embarrassed to buy it myself. At 20 years old, I had no business tending to a plant, let alone, a child. It should also be noted that to this day, I still cannot grow plants - all the more reason, not to have a child.

I'd eventually shared the news with Dude. Before he could process that bombshell, I then told him that I was not keeping it. All of a sudden, his stoicism turned to anger. He'd said that if I went through with "that" I'd never have to worry about him ever speaking to me again. Dude also said he wasn't going to give me any money for the termination, nor was he going to take me to San Diego for the procedure. "Good luck figuring it out", he spat, just before he left my barracks room, and slammed the door. Dude was always dismissively cruel, but I'd hoped he'd muster up a little empathy, given the circumstances. He did not.

Realizing I'd have to figure this out on my own, I picked up the phone, and called my mother in Maryland. It was already well into the night in California, so it was in the wee hours of the morning back home. "Is everything alright?" she'd asked, groggily. My voice shaking, I'd replied: "umm, I got myself in a little bit of trouble." "What kind of trouble?"
I responded in quiet sobs. The way my mother said "Oh no" over the phone, to this day, breaks my heart. You could hear the disappointment in her voice. "I don't have money to pay, and the guy said he won't help me, how could I be so stupid? I can't keep this baby! My life is ruined!" By this time, I'd burst into a full sob. "Ok, ok, ok..." Mom said quietly. "I will send the money by Western Union. It'll be alright." I profusely apologized for disappointing her, before getting off the phone.

I'd made some mistakes in my life, but this by far, was the biggest. All my so-called "friends" on the base scattered. None of them helped me. Suddenly, they "didn't want to get involved". I flirted with the idea of ending my own life. Figured something, anything, would be better than what I was facing. I went to the medicine cabinet looking for pills. All I could find was headache medicine. Fine, I thought. This should do the trick. I dumped an incalculable amount in my hand, and quickly put them in my mouth. I turned on the sink, and drank straight from the tap. Not much, but just enough to get the pills down. I went straight to bed, expecting not to wake up, having died in my sleep. Instead, I woke up the next morning with a terrible stomach ache. Realizing I'd been spared, I peeled myself off the bed, forced myself to vomit up the pills by sticking my finger down my throat, showered, and went into work as usual. I started making calls to local clinics, and arranged for a visit. El Centro at the time, didn't have an abortion clinic in town, so I'd have to go to San Diego to have it done. Back then, I was pulling down a whopping $1200/month in take home pay, so I couldn't afford a car. So I thought I'd take the Greyhound there. That plan, however, quickly dissolved, as the clinic in San Diego informed me that by law they couldn't release me to my own devices, post-procedure.

As the old saying goes though, God takes care of babies and fools, me being the latter. Word had gotten around base, and relative strangers came out of the woodwork to help me. A woman, with whom I was friendly, but not familiar, heard about my predicament. She herself didn't have a car, but she was friends with one of the Navy wives, and had already asked her if she would be willing to take me to San Diego. This woman, I had even less interaction with, decided to help me. That didn't matter to her. In her mind, she said "someone needed help, and if you can, you should help." We spoke briefly to work out the logistics. Eventually the day came, and she had I headed up to the clinic. I was calm, up until the actual procedure began. I was hysterical and had to be restrained. The last thing I remembered, was the burning sensation of anesthesia going into my veins. Terminating a pregnancy is an extremely emotional ordeal and damaging to the psyche. I carried the guilt and shame for years. I vowed to never put myself in such a position again.

After I returned to the base, I forged ahead as best I could. I'd see Dude in passing, but largely, we did a good job at avoiding each other. And that was fine with me. To add insult to injury, it was later revealed that he was also messing around with one of the other girls in the barracks; who was one floor below my room. Once I was no longer of use, he began seeing her openly. From my window, I'd see them; out and about. They were from the same state, and would regularly go on leave together. It was like a punch in the gut, every time. Even worse, she and I wound up in a fist fight, after she attacked me at work. I could only assume it was because she was upset about the pregnancy. This was also the last time I'd fought over a guy. There is a quote by Toni Morrison, in the book, When and Where I Enter that says: "She'd nothing to fall back upon [...] not anything [...] and out of the profound desolation of her reality she may well have invented herself."

I indeed had nothing to fall back on. No new man by which to be distracted. No alcohol. Only fragments of myself. I now know that periodically, things have to fall completely apart to clear the way for the next phase of life. Sure, trying to avoid it works for a time. But eventually the lesson will be learned. So I got busy, stitching myself back together.

As mentioned before, I'd gone into the Navy without a designated rate/specialty. Sometime shortly after I'd gotten to the base, the Command Master Chief (CMC), with my service record in hand, sat me down, and asked me what I'd intended to do with myself. To clarify, the CMC served as a liaison between the Commanding Officer and the enlisted members of the base, so was custom for them to make such inquiries. At the time, I said "do my 4 and get out." My ASVAB (Armed Services Vocational Aptitude Battery) score was abysmally low; I barely scored high enough to get in, let alone qualify for any technical schooling. So I masked my fear and shame of this fact, with cynicism. But he would have none of it. "You could take it over, and see if you can get a better score." I eventually agreed to do so. I'd figured since I had 3 years left, I'd better start taking my career seriously, and get my shit together. He'd made arrangements for me to go TDY (Temporary Duty) to Naval Station San Diego for one month. During which time, I took remedial classes, learned proper study techniques, applied them and re-took the exam. This time, I'd scored high enough to qualify for a number of technical schools. I'd chosen Radioman 'A' school. It was about five months long, and much to my chagrin, in Great Lakes, Il. The same place I'd gone to boot camp just 2 years prior. This would prove to be a reoccurring theme in my life: moving on from some place, only to return again. I'd have to wait on a class convening date, before I could be permanently transferred. While I was waiting, I decided to start exercising and eating better. I could regularly be found walk/running around the base in the evening just before sundown. I started reading and writing more. I distanced myself from the drinking. By this time, I'd also purchased a 1993 Geo Prism. So, I regularly visited the new friends I'd made up in San Diego.

Eventually, my transfer orders came in. I had about 2 weeks to get from California to Illinois. I'd gotten a AAA membership, and one of their agents was kind enough to create a flip-chart map of the entire trip, which was just over 2000 miles. Given that I lived in the barracks, I didn't have any large furniture to move. So I packed that Geo Prism to the gills, and began my cross country drive. Just before I left the base, I filled up my gas tank, and happened upon Dude. Holding true to his promise, he avoided eye contact, and didn't say a word. I responded in kind. I left quietly with full intent on never looking back.

This was pre-GPS days. I had only the good Lord, and the AAA map, by my side. I drove through places with peculiar names: Tucumcari. Gallup. Joplin. I drove all day, stopping only to fill up on gas and get food. Once it got dark, I found a hotel to rest up for the next day. Eventually, I arrived safely to Great Lakes. It took me 3 ½ days.

Classes started almost immediately. Because there were so many students, classes were split into day and evening sessions: 6am-12pm, 12pm-6pm. I'd been assigned the 6am, which meant I had to get up at 430am. As I'd fallen into yet another routine, I'd no time to lament over what occurred at my last duty station. Five months went by rather quickly, and it was time, yet again, to select another duty station. I was given 3 choices; from the three, I picked Keflavik, Iceland. And this was how it went. I would be stationed somewhere for a time, and then get assigned somewhere else. After Iceland, I went to a merchant marine ship. After there, I went on yet another ship. I'd come to appreciate the Navy, and would re-enlist for another 3 years. With all the moving around, the pain of California slowly become a distant memory.

Around 2000, while onboard my last ship, a whole 3 years after I'd left El Centro, something strange happened. Dude tracked me down. I left no forwarding address and did not keep in touch with anyone after I left the 1st duty station, so I'm not even sure how he found out where I was. He was stationed on one of the air craft carriers in Norfolk, VA, and he'd been trying to find me.
    "I'm just gone' say it. Hay I'm real sorry for the way I did you back then. You ain't deserve that", he said.
Dude told me he married to the woman he'd began seeing (the one I'd gotten into a fight with). While he was out to sea, she wrote him the dreaded "Dear John" letter – which was the worst thing a spouse can do to someone while they are out to sea. He continued, "man you know she turned around and did me the same way. I never understood how you felt, until it was done to me."
I didn't know what to say. I expressed that fact. He and the woman had since begun the process of divorce, but not before having 2 children.
"I suppose you got the children you always wanted, huh", I'd said.
"Yeah. But you did the right thing for yourself."
That I did. The child would not have been conceived in love, and I'd only be repeating the pattern I came from. It just wasn't worth it. The conversation lasted less than 5 minutes, ending with an awkward, "take care". I never expected anything from him, let alone an apology. I hung up, feeling a strange sense of gratitude. I received an apology, a reconciliation of my pain. I suppose is more than some people (who've experienced far worst) get.
    When I think of the experience in California, it ranks high as one of the lowest points of my life. However; grief and pain are strange bedfellows. On the surface, they come to destroy, but, at the same time they force motivation for radical self-improvement, that we would otherwise, not seek out for ourselves. Things have to fall completely apart, in order to come together again – so we can learn the lesson. Or maybe so the other parties can learn a lesson. Had I not gone through that experience, would I have been roused from my complacency with

my Naval career? Would I have acknowledged the interconnectedness of mine, and my mothers' stories? Or that fatherlessness did have a profound effect on my life? Would I have finally taken the time to go to therapy, and learn to build a solid plan of self-care? Would I have witnessed the humanity and kindness of others? Would I have learned how to respect my finite amount of energy? Probably not, things happened the way they did for a reason.

And, as Pema Chodron asserts: "only to the extent that we expose ourselves over and over to annihilation can that which is indestructible in us be found." In the midst of complete annihilation, we can indeed, discover our own indestructibility.

CHAPTER TWO

The Triumph of the Unshakable Grief

    I want to start this chapter off by saying life is so interesting. Life often throws us curveballs, and unexpected occurrences, that we don't think we're going to make it through. I think grief falls into that category, it's something no one really expects and often has an unpredictable outcome. Honestly, when I think of grief, I think of someone dying or leaving this earth. What I've realized is grief is so much more than that; it's something we experience on different levels, at different times and in many variations. Grief has the ability to shape who we are, it can determine where we're headed and if left undealt with, it can change what we think about ourselves. My grief story is just as pertinent as yours. You will read this chapter and wonder exactly how I made it through and how my life changed. I intend to clearly lay that foundation for you. I hope this chapter helps you understand that there's nothing in life you can't overcome if you're committed to walking through it.

    I've learned to call myself the comeback kid because I have been knocked down more times than I would have ever liked to; but, I realize I've always come back stronger by the grace of God. So as you read this chapter, I hope it resonates with you and you identify with some of the things I'm talking about. I want to encourage you to keep going, and know you're not alone. Know that we are all grieving on different levels, and that once we get through the processes, life goes pretty smooth. Life has a funny way of shifting and from all of the things that have happened in my life I realize that you just go to sleep, keep getting up, and one day the sun begins to shine.

    I've never been able to share all of me with anyone. I've always masked so much of myself because I get wrapped up and lost in the motions, forgetting who I am and how far I've come. In my mind, I've always had to be strong or at least carried on that façade. At one point, no one knew all my secrets or truths because I didn't know if they could handle it. The little truths I do have make things awkward and utterly confusing so I know sharing too much is a no go especially with those close to me. As

I've grown to understand my truth. I've become a woman that is confident in who I am, what made me, and how I'm supposed to carry out my life. That is my progress. I am destined to tell it all, bear my soul and leave my truth. Once you know me, you know me, and you will know that my life is pretty much your life, mirrored, in different parts and pieces.

I believe God is the only entity that knows me to the core. He is the creator, the Alpha and the Omega, the beginning and the end. However, He brings people in your life who will know you though Him. Your spouse may be one these people. They're a direct reflection of you, in most cases. When you're strong or an extrovert many think you're the strongest person ever, but honestly, you may think you're weak because you feel beat down and worn out a lot. Now, of course my perspective has changed over time, but I give you these feelings and these thoughts or interpretations, so you can understand the world that I came from. I think I get weaker as time goes on because my dependence isn't on me – it's on my heavenly father and I need that. I try not to make excuses for myself or hold on to my issues. It took me a long time to understand that all issues have to be dealt with, and I had to grieve my losses. Life isn't meant to be pushed under the rug. Eventually, it'll get exposed. Grief is something that ultimately never leaves us but gets easier as time passes.

Truth is –views and grief go hand-in-hand. We grieve simply because we've been abused in areas. We have holes we haven't filled, and they need to be packed. What we pack them with matters the most. We grieve because we've lost important pieces of our lives that we cannot replace. We also grieve because something or someone has left us and they will never come back.

Grief set in for me at an early age when my parents. They undoubtedly were loves of my life. I watched them fight, and divorce. I remember each fight because I was constantly in the middle. I was forced to pick a side it seemed and unbeknownst to them, I definitely felt like I had to be loyal to someone. But, how could I be loyal to either of them when I loved them both? I also hated them at the same time. I hated what they had turned into. I hated that I was lost. I spent time with my grandma, and she was my rock. Make no mistake my grandma, dad, stepmom, and my biological mom were all forces to be reckoned with and they played vital roles in my life. Growing up, my mom was feisty, a firecracker to say the least. She had a bit of a temper, and sometimes I just so happened to be on the wrong end of that stick. I realized my parents did the best they could with what they had, and in the heat of the moment, they took things out on me. It didn't make it right, nor did it make it acceptable; but it absolutely made it true! I lived with that for years; mental, emotional, and physical abuse at the hands of loved ones. Now, because of who I am I didn't make the situation better. I, too, was feisty; a firecracker and a force to be reckoned with. And so, my grief started from dealing with the loss of my relationship with her (mom) to having to alter my relationship with him (dad) to satisfy everyone.

Then I looked at the people closest to me and determined they were the two people that probably hurt me the most. As life went on, my world was shaped by these incidents of the past that would lead into my future. I became immensely submerged into boys, my sexuality, and my physical appearance. Dealing with childhood sexual abuse forced me to grieve the little girl inside of me. I grew up faster than many of my peers. I valued my physical appearance and I looked at it as an asset. I knew I was amazingly gorgeous, but I was wondering exactly how that would work out for my benefit because emotionally I was so broken. Luckily, I was not a promiscuous person; but mentally, I definitely thought I was somewhere in between. I lost who I was because that person essentially died, but I wanted to have the relationship that had left. I wanted to make it right and fix me but was ill-equipped. I hooked up with this guy, and we ended up having a child. Our lives were toxic together, and I ultimately ended up leaving, but not before the rest of me was shattered. I will say that my life changed during those days, and nights. By the time I had my son, that abusive relationship took control over me. Wanting to leave, desiring to be free, I left to try and figure out who I was and how to get back to me. I didn't have time though. I mean, how could I? I was a full-time mom, full-time worker, full-time student, and I didn't have time to figure out what my identity was. I knew my name, what I wanted to become, and I knew what I didn't want to become. That drove me for much of my life. Statistically, I had a baby at 17 and was supposed to fail. I worked my butt off, I moved on again to a new relationship which led to marriage, and thought all was well. I didn't have any more children until after grad school, and I seemed to be the model girl, right? I proved them all wrong. I thought things were going well! My now ex-husband and I didn't fight, we seemed to compromise well, and we seriously had a beautiful family. We churched together, served together, and had all the best friends. And just like that - it was over. Overnight - it was done. It was like nothing I had ever seen before.

    I married at 19, such a young tender age. Serenaded by this 21 year old man, we dated for about 4 months. I just knew he was it! Grief initiates rebound because it draws you toward an unlikely conclusion that is based on emotion. Truth be told, the person I wanted to be with was unavailable. Instead of me waiting and staying the course, I needed and craved a relationship because grief gives you a false sense of stability. One thinks they've handled something that takes years and many processes to actually process. My ex and I had very different backgrounds and many different cultural and moral beliefs, but hey love is love right? WRONG! Fast forward, we were married 2 months later, without anyone knowing what we had done. I thought it was the best thing ever but that soon changed. I soon realized - there were several problems. For one, I learned about 8 months later; he had been in infidelity with multiple women. I found myself truly devastated, but willing to work hard for my marriage. I stayed. This toxic part of my life caused all sorts of issues from alcoholism and abuse, to breach of trust, disease, and deceit. I wondered who this person was and what had I done. I simply focused on being a better me, and I presumed he had done the same. As life moved on; I continuously grieved who I had become. This once vibrant women had become an angry resentful person. I tried to piece it together and move on. I came to learn that he was built differently than me. Our minds never really synced, and what I called a dominant personality, he called controlling. What he said was a passive personality, I called weakness. This created underlining issues that truthfully I didn't comprehend.

As I look back at it - communication was a struggle on his end and maybe on mine too. I thought we did the best we knew how. This, of course, was not to bash him and for some I'll spare the nasty details, but divorce killed me. We had a daughter after two years, saved loads of money, took trips, had our ministry, life was restored, I thought. One day, after what I thought was five years of bliss; he deployed. Seven days later, he left. We were in love on a Sunday at 12pm, and he was essentially done with our life, our family, and me by 7:30pm. This is when life turned into a nightmare. The person I thought I married was no more and man, did I go through hell! He made sure my life was as complex as possible. He cut all ties with "my" kids (as he called them), he stopped any financial assistance (while I was in school FT, he cleaned out our bank accounts, cancelled life insurance policies, and took my 401K savings. My so-called friends stopped dealing with me (maybe I wasn't the nicest), and I became sick - mentally, emotionally, and physically. I looked at my kids daily as they asked about their dad who wanted nothing to do with them. I was broke, disgusted, blamed for it all, and left incredibly broken. Dead.

Suddenly, he turned his infidelity into mine. He began to flaunt his indiscretions on social media in front of me. Many of the people I loved knew things that I didn't know. For the record, I NEVER stepped out on my spouse - but that wasn't his story. Life was in shambles for me. I spent 8 months of pure hell to get a divorce that I didn't think I wanted. He was relentless with his lies and spiteful at his finest. Now, I had a decision to make - high road or low wave. I went high as much as I could. I cried through every church service and with every friend. I couldn't sleep or eat, and I physically couldn't move many days. I went through major depression and anxiety. Yet instead, I stayed above the water as much as I could. I'm human, and it was tough. But, I kept at it knowing that God would settle up eventually. The years were long and my ex didn't make anything easy or good. In actuality and to this day, he has no involvement with my kids, and he still goes out of his way to make things difficult.
However, life has a funny way of working things out. I absolutely

thought I was paying for some sort of bad decision I had made in my youth.

Two months after I divorced, I was sexually assaulted. In the city I had moved to and lived in for 10 years. I was deeply hurt. I didn't know if I was coming or going. I couldn't understand what was happening in my world and why this was happening. I was attempting to live my life after this divorce, and it just seemed so complicated. How did going to the store turn into a sexual assault? Everything in my world shifted and at that moment, I thought I was going to die. I wasn't sure what was happening, and I had no control of what was happening. It appeared that my world had crashed. All I could think about was my kids and my parents. I couldn't bear to know that that would be the last time they would see me. I could not think this was the way I was going to go out. What would this person even do to me? It was terrible in a way that no woman or man should experience.

On that day, death and grief rocked me. Divorce changed my spirit, rape destroyed my soul. I lived in torment. I thought it was my fault. I wondered what I could have done differently. I asked myself was I strong enough to endure. How was I going to make it after that? As a looked myself in the mirror for days, the marks, bruises, the aches and pains, the visits to the doctors, the pills and humiliation – I lost me. I lost who I was, and I knew I was no longer Kyla. Every ounce of me that could've been left was gone. It was hard for me to accept. I went to counseling, and I tried to put myself back together, but I just couldn't do it. I realized that the only thing that was going to be able to do it was time; time is this thing we all have. We all believe time will heal everything that we've been through. In actuality, the only thing that heals us of our pain and grief is absolutely walking through our processes. The moments that we have from the good to the bad are all in the details. We can't live our lives from the highest mountain. We must get down into the lowest points, peeks, and valleys to really see what is happening. Grief requires us to hit the lowest pain point and work upward. In other words, we aren't allowed to sit in the agony that grief creates. We are required to push past our comfort zone and deal with the intriguing details of life.

When I went through my divorce years ago, I went through a series of other events as mentioned. Months after divorce, I was sexually assaulted, boarder line homeless, and I had to send my kids away while maintaining doctorate studies. I took a lower paying job and sold everything I had. It seemed like it wouldn't turn around. I took time to myself for about a year. I went through what seemed like public shame and all my relationships suddenly changed.

I pursued my education and managed to stay on track. Through all the highs and even more lows one day life turned around. I started a business, wrote a book, started dating, and began walking in my purpose. I travelled more, saw the beauty in second chances, and I saw God in a whole new light. It seemed like every time something great happened I was forced to deal with a huge distraction, but for the most part I started to really figure out how life was going to work. Now, I'm not saying that I understood how life worked in every form, but I understood the distractions around me. When we talk about grief to grind we must recognize, that they are in two totally different categories, but they're intertwined to give us an outcome.

Your grind has to surpass your grief. It has to surpass every piece of you down to the fiber of your being. It has to dig deep in order for you to get to a place where you're sick and tired of being sick and tired. Then, you decide that you're going to take your grief by the horns and command it to get it together. That was my grind. My grind was saying that I wasn't going to be what society said I should have been. I was not going to be a bitter black woman. I wasn't going to be a broken woman. I was not going to be a victim. And, I was not going to sit there and die! I was not going to grieve for the rest of my life. I was going to discover who I was, what I was, and figure out how Kyla was supposed to move forward in life.

That is what I did. I decided I was going to turn my tragedies into victories. I decided that life was absolutely what I made it, and I was determined not to become my circumstances. I am absolutely my decisions. I am my choice, and I absolutely have that choice to be great. Of course, this comes with hard work and peeling back loads of layers. It's trying to understand who you are, where you are, and what happens from there. I mention that a lot because that's a question that you have to constantly ask yourself. Who am I? Where am I going and what do I want? I had to realize that I am absolutely in control of my destiny. I may not be in control of what happens to me or what someone does to me, but I am absolutely in control of my responses. I realize that in life all we have is the grind. All we have are our moments in between moments where we have to wake up and make a decision. In life we absolutely have time for every single thing that we want. We put each to-do item on the scale and some things come before others. We have to be OK with that. When talking about grief, grief comes in various forms, but it always goes through the same steps. There's always a moment where we have to embrace it, accept it, and we have to live it. We have to try to get back on track with it. When we're talking about grief, we have to realize that there's a certain way that we are going to cope with life. It means there are things that we have issues to resolve.

The grind is very similar because we have to continue to work through all of those things because we want to see results right? For every single person that has been through grief or is grieving the loss of themselves, others, situations, etc. the question is how do you get through it? How do you impose new results? How do you accept your grief and turn it into your grind?

The world is strange because when feelings are involved things seem to take a turn. We're emotional. When I get in my feelings usually it's because I think my life is jacked up, and I need to fix another person's life instead. I am just a woman. I struggled in my career because I wanted to be something to help other people not become what I ultimately thought I was. I wanted to be a coach because I knew how it felt to not have it together and be so disturbed. I knew the negative mindset and the distractions and disruptions that came. I liked to be in control because I've been out of control. I knew it wasn't easy; but mentally, sometimes I am screwed up. The physical abuse I've endured made me extra hard on my physical appearance because I've seen it bloody and bruised. The way I critique my face, lips, hair, and skin is because I have flashbacks of busted lips, bruised cheeks, and broken blood vessels. I knew what it was like to be told I'm ugly and made fun of and no matter how confident I was in myself. The confidence doesn't change the abuse I've dealt with.

Two ways to get new results: You accept your grief and you live for your grind. What exactly does that mean? It means you're going to embark upon this journey, you're going to accept your truth, and go for it. You're going to prepare for the truth in whatever capacity that is. Oftentimes, we are still grieving because we've yet to accept and walk-through what that looks like. Ultimately, we have no choice. We have to walk out every facet of our life to the best of our abilities if we ever want to see the grind. The grind does not necessarily have to be the hustle, bustle, and the struggle. The grind is simply getting results. The grind can be increase; the grind can be an enlargement of territory; it can be healing. The grind is being able to look back on your blood, sweat, and tears and see the fruit of your life and your labor. It all seems so hard at times, but it's very, very practical. You can break it down in as many steps as you want to simplify it.

I choose to simplify, and I choose to simplify that for you all to live your truth, be empowered in your truth, share your truth, and heal from your truth! If you manage to do these four things, I promise you that your grind will always be sweet because you're always going to be passionate about it. You'll always be learning. You'll always be inspired to see results. You'll realize that your priorities are intact when you really grind. I am encouraging you to sit down and write out how you're trying to embrace your truth and your grief. Feel everything that you need to feel about every situation, every hurt, every heartache, every disappointment, and in every dismissive thing that could ever disappoint you; you have to feel that pain, fear, and resentment. In order for you to move forward in your life with your grind you must know where grief hits you. It will make you feel like pushing. It propels and moves us forward.

When it comes to grief we need a few things. The number one thing we need in this life to be effective is growth. The second thing is truth. The third thing is the determination to continue the journey while bringing the first two things together.

I caution anybody who just decides they're going to put a situation behind them and never deal with it. Don't lock your grief in a box with the key and bury it because you'll become a hostage to it. Take the box out no matter how heavy it is, no matter how hard it is, no matter how rested it is. Be sure to find the key, unlock the box, and pull the contents out.

CHAPTER THREE

Death of Me

Relationships are like a dance, with visible energy racing back and forth between the partners. Some relationships are the slow, dark dance of death.
~Colette Dowling

Loss of Value

I was driving in traffic down an intense, one-way road---speeding like someone driving a getaway vehicle after a bank robbery. I was pregnant; probably 4-5 months. My mind was not even on the life that was developing in me. My mind was dangerously focused on my soon-to-be husband. Dodging oncoming traffic, swerving in and out of lanes, and cutting off cars by less than an inch of the bumper. I was senselessly determined to chase him down that one-way road.

We had just finished arguing. It didn't matter whether I was right or wrong or if we could've ever reached a compromise. His rebuttal was always, "I wouldn't have these problems if I had a white woman". It was always stated jokingly, but I knew in my spirit, he meant it. In moments like those, a feeling of insecurity seemed to creep throughout my mind. I couldn't even remember why we started arguing. I knew I was the one to beg, plead, cry, and have an absolute fit when he left or threatened to leave. *It was sick and dysfunctional*. At the time, I was too naïve, inexperienced, and confused about my own identity to know that I was sowing seeds into barren land.

This was the situation I found myself in. A high-speed case for a runaway dysfunctional love. It was fifteen minutes after five in the evening. It was starting to get dark earlier because of daylight savings time. The driver's window was rolled down, and I was smoking my favorite stress-relieving vice. A Newport Long. Now when I look back, it's hard to believe that my mind frame was underneath the barrel. Not at the bottom. UNDERNEATH IT! I realize now that I had a destructive mindset and unhealthy behavioral habits towards my relationship with men. When it came to women, I rarely trusted any.

Thirty-eight years later, two marriages, one divorce, two kids, many failed relationships, emotional draining traumatic events, and no concept about self-worth, value, self-care, and accountability TO SELF...I've learned a great deal. I've learned that even though I was the victim of many things, the biggest victimization I experienced is being a victim of self-destruction.

I committed murder, but it was justified. I had to kill myself so I could live again, except this time, the abundant way of living.
~Nicole Redmond

People often equate grief to losing a love one. A loved one could be a child, mother, father, brother, sister, best friend, or even a pet. I remember reading an article about different types of grief and it mentioned, even before our birth, we begin experiencing loss. We are literally born into the world with an identification of who we are tied to another human being. The common denominator of grief that everyone will experience at one time or another is the holistic action of loss. Grief is a journey to show you who you really are in seasons of loss. *I committed murder, but it was justified. I had to kill myself so I could live again, except this time; I needed to live the abundant way.* An article published on Oprah Winfrey's website under inspiration and written by Dr. Kenneth J. Doka, expressed the three kinds of grief nobody talks about. The most powerful statement in that article said, "Grief is not always about death, but it is always about attachment and separation".

Attachment! Separation! Grief! Loss! Death! And, co-dependency. The number one factor each of these has in common is "bond". The person experiencing a loss once was "attached" to the object and have experienced a forced "separation". When someone grieves over another, they have a strong bond with that object or person. Whether that bond is healthy or unhealthy, functional or dysfunctional, it provides a garden of characteristics that make up someone with codependent behaviors if not effectively balanced.

But....what happens when you lose someone intentionally? Meaning, you participated in their death. You lose them because that person was destructive in every aspect of your mental, spiritual, and emotional growth and being. BUT….you loved them, or you loved the idea that you believed they needed you. You couldn't imagine being without them. Yet, in the same breath, you hated them for who they really were and what they've contributed to you *becoming*.

Loss of Healthy Reasoning & Voice

My sister-in-law, from my first marriage, mentioned the word co-dependency to me visiting our home one evening. Her husband and five kids were enjoying their visit. The adults were downstairs talking. I was in the kitchen as usual, preparing some food for everyone, but still engaging the conversation. It was during a time when her brother and I were experiencing continuous marital strain. We were all talking about a television show. I disagreed with my husband on a statement he made. I didn't think anything of it. I briefly left the kitchen to go to the bathroom in our master suite. When I was done, I walked back into the bedroom, and he was standing in the middle of the room in the front of our bed with a crazed look on his face.

He walked into my personal space so that his face was direct with mine. He whispered in a stern and annoyingly stressed voice, saying, "I don't need my sister looking at me like I don't know what I am talking about. So, the next time you have something to say and you don't agree with what I am saying, keep your fucking mouth shut". Immediately I took defense as I tried to process the logic to a response I was not anticipating.

My initial reaction was, "What? What are you talking about?" "Don't act stupid. You know what I am talking about. All you need to do it fix some fucking food and shut the hell up. Can you do that?"

He immediately left the room and closed the door behind him. I began crying intensely and tried to muffle my sobs as to not let his family hear my *grief*. I went in the bathroom to gather myself. I convinced myself that since he was older than me he knew best. He was married before. He had my best interest and he needed me as a wife. Most importantly, and one of the main destructive principles I based my marriage on was *I didn't want my child to grow up without having both parents in her life like I did.* Great idea, but bad combination.

> ***Codependents may exhibit the characteristics of a caretaker. They:***
> 1. ***Think and feel responsible for other people – for other people's feelings, thoughts, actions, choices, wants, needs, well-being, lack of well-being, and ultimate destiny.***
> 2. ***Feel anxiety, pity, and guilt when other people have a problem.***
> 3. ***Find themselves saying yes when they mean no, doing things they don't really want to be doing, doing more than their fair share of the work, and doing things other people are capable of doing for themselves.***

    I walked back into the living room area trying my best to hide what I was mentally experiencing. It seemed his sister was attuned to my sorrow because her eyes were on me as I quietly walked to the kitchen. About twenty minutes passed before the men were fully engaged in an all-out roaring discussion on football. My sister-in-law walked in the kitchen and asked if I had a couple of free minutes to go out in the front of the house. We talked for a long time about various things, but before we went back inside she said, "Nicole, when you get some time look up the word codependent". I replied with a questionable, "OK". I didn't look it up.

Loss of Identity
One of the main reasons I joined the military was to get away from my parents' home. Germany was my first duty location in the Army. One the *many* guys I dated during this time in my life name was Carey. We lived in co-ed barracks on the third floor. He was short, fair-skinned, black guy. He had jet black, curly hair. The biggest smile and devil-charm. When he took care of his hair, it was styled in a neat fade. For the most part, he kept it unruly and rouge looking. He was funny, edgy, and wild. We dated for a brief time. We broke up after I caught him in the act of sexual acrobatics with a German lady.

I remember banging on his door like a crazy person daring him to come out of his barracks room. Thinking back, I can easily say that I was a hot mess, but the reality was I didn't know anything about loving myself. I had been hurt from outside forces and my internal being was consistently being traumatized because I lacked self-love. I thought I needed to be loved from external forces. For a long time, I labeled myself as a barracks whore. Crazy, I know! By this time, women were becoming more prominent about their sexual liberties. Though that movement was and still is one of free expression of owing one's own body completely. During that time, anytime I saw or heard about the statement "turning a hoe into a house wife", I felt it applied to me. This was how I saw myself by the age of eighteen. My nickname I gave myself was Queen B. The "B" was not for Beyoncé. Today, all I can say is thank God for growth, seeking to be delivered from my other self, and applying healthy habits to my thought-process that dismantled the characteristics of poor relationship habits and an unhealthy ideal about self.

Codependents may exhibit characteristics of dependency, by:
1. *Feeling terribly threatened by the loss of anything or person they think can provide happiness.*
2. *Constantly seeking love from people incapable of loving*
3. *Desperately seek love and approval.*
4. *Not taking time to see if other people are good for them.*
5. *Centering their lives around other people.*
6. *Tolerating abuse to keep people around them.*

Loss of Freedom of Body & Support System
Until I officially left home, most of my early teen years were spent in Tampa, Florida. When I was twelve, I recall going back home to New York one time to visit my dad after we moved. At the time, my mom had recently purchased her first home with her boyfriend in a new neighborhood in Palms Country, Florida. During our first year living there, I often

overheard my mom and Mr. Reggie talk about bringing his son over from South America.

After a few years, Paul officially came to live with us. Paul was Mr. Reggie's son. My mom and Mr. Reggie still were not married at the time (this was going on approximately 8 years). Unfortunately, I don't remember the details of our relationship up until the point that Paul inappropriately fondled me. Paul was two years older than me, dark-skinned, and nearly two inches shorter than me. His fingernails were embedded in his skin from excessive biting which I thought was disgusting.

It was late evening and both my mom and Mr. Reggie were in the room with their door closed on the other side of the house. My brothers were in the house doing God knows what. I just opened the door to my room which was diagonal to my brothers' room. As soon as I was half way in my room, Paul comes in behind me and closed the door. He covered my mouth and aggressively started to put his right hand down my pants. He reached my private area and then inserted his disgusting fingers inside of me and penetrated me several times. He backed up off me and started to exit my room. I immediately fixed my pants and went after him in a violent rage.

I started hitting him in his back and screaming to the top of my lungs, "how could you? How could you!?" My mom and Mr. Reggie hastily came out of their room. I was screaming and crying trying to say a coherent statement about what took place. My mom saw I was in some form of distress. I walked towards them both and passed them and proceeded to their room. I calmed myself down enough to speak clearly. "Paul, he touched me inappropriately", I said nervously. "What?" my mom replied angrily. "She's lying, Kay", Mr. Reggie stated in defense. "I am not lying!" I replied, confused and upset. I ran over to Mr. Reggie and immediately started to hit him. Repeatedly screaming at the top of my lungs, "I am not lying!"

By then, my mother had pulled me off Mr. Reggie and yelled at me to go into my room. I looked at her as if she betrayed the United States and used me to do it. I ran out of their room, outside the front door, and down the street to the neighbor's house. I ran so fast I was out of breath and hysterically banging on the door. Mrs. Jacobs answered the door questioning me. She invited me in her home and started to hug me and comfort me. I couldn't bear to tell her what happened. After a couple of minutes, she gave me a towel and instructed me to take a shower and lie down.

Codependents may exhibit characteristics of low self-worth:
1. *Come from troubled, repressed, and dysfunctional homes.*
2. *Feel different than the rest of the world.*
3. *Fear rejection.*
4. *Have been victims of sexual, physical, or emotional abuse; neglect, abandonment, or alcoholism.*

Acceptance

Growing up, I was the caretaker for my two twin brothers while my mom worked in Manhattan. We had a babysitter for the most part. However, I cared for them, prepped dinner before my mother got home and made sure the house was in order. I was also sexually curious before the age of ten. I lost my virginity at the age of thirteen and increasingly became more sexually active. I lied and stole like a petty city thief. I was a young con artist. I am not proud of the things I did growing up, but I didn't know the things I lacked during my childhood was the reason for my poor decision-making skills when it came to relationships.

I witnessed men coming in and out of my mom's life until Mr. Reggie decided to stay. I also don't recall my parents ever divorced. My most peaceful memories of my dad was him picking my brothers and I up every other weekend to be taken to the Bronx to spend time with our other family. Every Sunday after church, my dad would stop by White Castle and buy at a minimum of 50 cheeseburgers. We would listen to the sound of my father's contiguous laughter and eat like a tribe of warriors. I have no bad memories of my father.

I could blame my mother for lacking to provide me the nurturing attention that I so needed. I could blame the various men that were temporarily part of my life who tried to play the daddy role to get into my mother's bed. I could blame the apartment I lived in growing up in the city. I could blame all the guys I gave myself to during my early teens before my first marriage. I could blame my ex-husband. I could blame my dad for not being around. There are many people, things, and situations I could place blame on for my long list of poor decision making. However, **blaming doesn't provide healing, just sustained hurt.** The blame eventually spiraled into my codependent behaviors over the years.

It wasn't until my second marriage with my current husband that I realized I might have characteristics of co-dependency. We decided to see a counselor for martial problems we were experiencing. During the session, the counselor was hard on my husband because the case was presented from the beginning that the problem was him. The session ended extremely bad. My husband stormed and left me there defending his behavior.

I started to get up and run after him, and the counselor said, "Mrs. Redmond, where are you going?"

I responded with an immediate, "After my husband".

Ms. Jones asked, "Why? Why are you going after him?"

I had no explanation. Then the question came back up again.

"Mrs. Redmond, have you ever heard of the word co-dependency?"

"Yes, yes I heard of that word through my studies. I am familiar with the word."

"Good, then you should know that you are codependent"

She grabbed a pen and paper to write on. She recommended me a book, *Codependent No More: How to Stop Controlling Others and Start Caring for Yourself* by Melody Beattie. It was several months before I got the book and read it. Immediately after the first two chapters, I put the book down and said to myself, *Lord, that's me* and began to weep uncontrollably. I had my first genuine breakthrough on understanding my unwanted relationship habits.

During my life to date, I have experienced a great deal of relational issues whether internal or external. Today, I am still married, by the grace of God, and every day I am still learning how to break codependent habits developed over the course of my life. For me to heal and discover genuine self-love, I had to consistently seek the "patterns" of problems that led to my destructive relationship behaviors. Therefore, I had to kill my old self and learn who I really was and that alone has been a grieving and victorious process and journey. The bottom line was I didn't have many good examples of familial relationships.

  A lack of nurturing and foundational family unit structure led to poor familial relationships. A lack of respected fatherly presence led to poor relationships with men. A lack of self-love led to naïve vulnerabilities in unrealistic relationships. A lack of unhealthy relationship skills led to unhealthy martial relationships. A lack of self-worth led to a codependent mindset and behaviors. This was my pattern. This was why, at the time, my marriage was in the volcanic stages of eruption. This was why my relationship with my daughter was unhealthy and consisted of hollering and screaming. This was why, until recently, I was unable to forgive my mother, Mr. Reggie, Paul and everyone else that contributed to my unknown history of dysfunctional relationship habits. I accepted the seeds and patterns that contributed to my ideal responses to relationships and begin the long process of self-discovery, self-acceptance, self-love, and self-sustainment.

  Acceptance is now part of my daily practice. Acceptance is also parallel with deliverance. I've peacefully accepted what is and understand what can and can't be changed and apply it daily. I have been delivered from an old way of doing something because the new way manifests growth. Acceptance is also one of the stages of the grieving process that was first identified by Elisabeth Kubler-Ross. The other stages have been experienced over the course of my life.

  I experienced ***denial*** in my marriages. As Melody Beattie describes, "We do everything and anything to put things in place or pretend the situation isn't happening". In the beginning stages of my second marriage, I experienced ***anger***. Understand at this point, I'd taken poor behaviors from my first marriage and indirectly applied them to my current marriage. I recall one time my husband had to explain to me, humbly *that he was not my first husband*. Even after I felt that he was genuinely compassionate about it, it was still some time before any change was met. With this anger, I was happy and raged at the loss of my first marriage. Everything that I did well was not acknowledged but met head-on with mentally degrading verbal assaults.

I experienced ***bargaining***. Attempting to postpone the inevitable and prevent a situation from happening. I often said to myself that if my spouse and I got counseling, then we wouldn't have to lose our relationship. See how that went. This became a coping mechanism, and if he didn't want to bargain I would have accepted the victim role again because I tried, and it didn't work.

I experienced ***depression***. I was clinically diagnosed with depression. Initially, it was very challenging because I didn't understand what was going on until I started coursework in Abnormal Psychology. Depression is the absolute darkest place of grief at its fullest. I MUST constantly seek the light in times like these. During this time, I gained a lot of weight after losing a great deal after my first marriage. I am still working to get it off. That's another battle for another story. I constantly sought to not be a victim of depression but an experienced survivor of its outcome.

It takes a great deal of universal well-being to love someone in absolute totality while still trying to figure out how to love yourself. I often recall many times, I would get annoyed in church when I heard people say, treat people how you want to be treated. My question was always…what if they don't know how to be treated? I never asked. I was attached to a reality that if a man loved me I would be good. I got so lost in my first marriage I detached from who I really was.

There was a quote I read somewhere that said: "we cannot begin to work on ourselves, to live our own lives, feel our own feelings, and solve our problems until we have detached from the object of obsession."

I was obsessed with wanting a marriage at any cost. I was obsessed with eating. I was obsessed with arguments. I was obsessed with being in pain. I was obsessed with lying. I was obsessed with everything that took the abundance of life away.

The most unaddressed passage of the acceptance stage is ***absolute forgiveness***. As it is often said that forgiveness is not for the person who hurts you, but forgiveness is for you. Most codependents grieve continuously and in unhealthy ways. Right now, if you are in a relationship of any sort, ask yourself...

What is this relationship allowing me to become? Is it something good or bad?

Killing Self

You may ask yourself the following questions.

1. How do I know if I am codependent?
2. What do I do first?
3. How do I determine I am if I am not sure?
4. How to I recover, survive, and live abundantly?

Acceptance looks different for everyone and can arrive at different times in one's life. I share with you four steps that will jump start your self-worth and dismantle characteristics and behaviors of co-dependency.

Step 1: Find and Identity your self-worth

In order to do this you must examine your current and past relationships, to include your childhood. What are your patterns? What does that look like? Was it traumatic? Was it healthy or unhealthy? How do those patterns contribute to who I am today? This moment of truth and peace may or may not be experienced in one point in time, but many points in time, at different moments and seasons.

These levels of mental inquiries will require an action and further inquiries until peace with solution is obtained.

The main purpose of doing this is to understand that your self-worth was at one point or another "abused" and you understand you do have positive self-worth that is waiting for ownership.

This is the most challenging stage for someone is simultaneously obtaining truth and peace. You can use tangible things such as professional counseling, journaling, talking to a confidant, volunteering, and or support groups. Once truth and peace have been obtained, you will be in the acceptance stage of the grieving process.

Step 2: Having steady mind-shift moments that create healthy habits

You will often hear life coaches talk about mindset. Mindset is a type of mind frame, i.e. Positive versus negative mindset. Mind-shift means mental and physical application of healthy habits manifested from a positive mindset. In *The Power of Habits: Why We Do What We Do In Life and Business,* Charles Duhigg reflects on Tony Dungy's philosophy about habits. Duhigg reveals that the key to an individual winning in life is changing their habits. We are creatures of habit. As Duhigg mentioned, habits can't be eradicated but must be replaced instead. To have a mind-shift moment you must understand in order to change an old habit, an old obsession must be addressed.

Whether you believe you are codependent or not, understanding the signs and symptoms of codependency can tremendously help. The following are areas of co-dependency. Each area has specific characteristics that delineates its symptoms. Those areas can be further explored in Melody Beattie's book. Caretaking, low self-worth, repression, obsession, control, denial, dependency, poor communication, weak boundaries, lack of trust, and anger.

I often say in general conversation that everyone has a mental health status. It depends on the level of imbalance that causes risk. People often joke about having OCD (Obsessive Compulsive Disorder), but if you have truly seen someone with this form of mental health concern you would understand the negative manifestation it can have on one's life. Tangible things that will enforce positive habits and a healthy mind-shift are: exercising, eating healthy, walking, joining empowering organizations, affirmations, and motivational speaking, to name a few.

Step 3: Having a spiritual practice

Now, a spiritual practice is not a religious domination. Do you love yourself enough to spend time alone with yourself? Having a spiritual practice enhances a deeper relationship with you. What greater way of honoring yourself than spending some peaceful time each day by ensuring you love you first. This is a challenge as well. Women often, by nature are nurturers. We can care for many others but exclude ourselves. A spiritual practice does not require religious belief.

Prayer is an outwardly expression and action of praise and acknowledgement to an outside external force. Prayer is very much required. Faith on the other hand, is an inwardly action expressed in physical manifestation with upfront physical evidence. Mediation is highly recommended because it is a practice of peace manifested in a continuous cycle of inward focus and outward purpose.

Step 4: Celebrating small wins

As you arrive at this crossroad in your journey, successfully navigating through the first three steps are necessary to celebrate your small wins. Small wins are accomplishing milestones that contribute to a specific goal. Being able to focus on the small and significant steps it takes to get to a goal are the small wins. An example of a small win is being able to wake in in the morning for 30 days straight and tell yourself positive affirmations that feed the spirit of your self-worth (step 1). Affirmations are speaking things into existence so it becomes a reality. Such as...
I am loved by me and I don't need any man's validation to be loved. My self-worth is priceless, so I should never attempt to sell it. My beauty is created by God and I love His creation. I am better than I was yesterday, and I am pleased with my soul

Every day that you wake up and accomplish an affirmation, you've just conquered a small win. A milestone to something great! Can you imagine being able to successfully do this for 30 days straight? You would accomplish a goal that you set out to do. Can you image what it would do to your mindset? There will be a shift and that shift will influence your behaviors (step 2).

(Beattie, 2001) (Duhigg, 2012)Some women might feel that they've endured years of abuse from self-destructive relationship habits and don't see how they can generate positive thoughts like affirmations. It is ok to feel like that. It is quite normal. However, it is not normal nor healthy to stay in that feeling. You can even celebrate small wins in being able to meditate or pray in a safe space daily (step 3). The main objective is to establish small wins that are centered around you moving pass the old you into the confident women God intended. Small wins are positive habits that are done constantly in order to build momentum towards greatness!

Resurrection and Rebirth
By implementing these steps, one has a greater possibility of not being a victim of codependency and having effective and healthy relationships with people. I know my boundaries. I am not in denial about who I am. I constantly seek truthful life lessons and apply them with a discerning spirit. I am flawed, but I accept my flaws as room to grow. Death is loss-we will never accept. By nature, we grieve. This grieving takes many shapes and many forms. By constantly seeking light, peace, and understanding of yourself, you gain a whole new mindset for the appreciation of life. People often want abundance but are not mentally and spiritually prepared for the struggle of growth. The struggle is real! But God's victories are not for the weak-hearted.

The abused me died sometime in 2015. The abundant me is continually being resurrected. People overlook a lot of biblical scriptures. One scripture says we are to crucify the flesh daily, while another one says we are to pick up our cross and follow the Lord daily. Another says that the spirit is willing but the flesh is weak. All these things are true. I sometimes envy the spirit of someone with greater obedience and discipline than mine. This is another tool I use to push myself to greatness. I often tell my clients that obedience is better than sacrifice when it comes to their finances or anything in life.

There were only two people at my funeral. The old me, lying in a casket and the new me, alive, and looking inside the casket. I have now accepted my loss in a way that has catapulted my success. Challenge yourself to seek purpose and live daily. Learn who you are daily. Celebrate your small wins. Be at peace with where you are and where you are headed.

Now in a bold and risky statement, I declare you to go and kill the destructive self. The purposed you is waiting for ownership!

For more information, or speaking engagements please contact me at holisticloveconquers@gmail.com

References

Beattie, M. (2001). *Codependent No More: How to Stop Controlling Others and Start Caring for Yourself.* Center City, Minnesota: Hazelden.

Doka, K. J. (n.d.). *3 Kinds of Grief That Nobody Talks About.* Retrieved from www.Oprah.com: http://www.oprah.com/inspiration/the-kinds-of-grief-nobody-talks-about

Duhigg, C. (2012). *The Power of Habit: Why We Do What We Do In LIfe and Business.* Random House.

CHAPTER FOUR

The Spirit Within Love Or Lust

What exactly is grief? I am sharing my truth about a form of grief, most of us don't even take a second thought about. My name is Phoenix J. Ma'ri, born Rochelle Johnson, but after my divorce, the Divine One (God) instructed me to change my name. I will take you through the seven stages of grief, well divorce grief, to include significant events which happened during this time. I will share how I was able to begin my process of healing, once I was able to identify where I was. This particular transition happened over a three year period, where I experienced not one, but three nervous breakdowns. Over the course, I realized the healing to help me overcome this idea, this facade of a lifestyle which I lived for so long, would not come from four walls, a denomination, or another person, but it would actually come from within me.

Are you ready to experience the pain, frustration, and grief of a woman whose love ran so deep, she lost her identity and became a woman she never thought she would become? Not only did she lose herself, but her mental capacity to accept the loss of her marriage drove her to a breakdown. She was able to rise from the ashes of these breakdowns, as a beautiful, divine, M.A.D., woman on a path lit with fire to show where she had traveled. Buckle your seat beats, the flight is about to begin.

Adjusting My Crown

Shock and Denial is the first stage of grief, but mines is entitled, Adjusting My Crown. I had to realize I was no longer the love of my soon-to-be ex-husband's. There is an institution, within a woman where she knows the man, especially if there is a spiritual, energetic connection, better than he knows himself. There was a feeling deep down inside of my heart, and I knew he was with someone else. Hell, I smelled her perfume on his shirt a few times. I didn't want to let it go. Phoenix was speaking to me, but due to me living inside of Rochelle's cave for so long, the voice of Phoenix was coming out in anger. I was in pure shock and denial, "What the fuck"?

I couldn't believe it was truly happening; he is with another woman. It appeared as though my whole world had reached a total stop. Here I was thinking we were taking a shot at things, and he was with her, but he was still mines. We were still married, and "How could he"? I knew deep down within my soul, this was wrong for feeling this way. How could I get mad, I filed for divorce.

I recall the first time the girls talked about meeting with this woman, he was going to bring into our life. Truly, I stated, "Our" in light of the fact that we were in the midst of the divorce and living separated. In my mind he belonged to me, the divorce was not final, and I was going to fight. For what? A position? What the hell was I thinking?

The reason this was unfitting to give up is we were still intimate. We were still messaging, sexting, and calling each other as though the divorce papers were not at the courts. He periodically would stop by for his lunch breaks, and we were even had lunch dates. I was considering these moments a gifts. I was having a piece of him, and this was well. However, the true issue is, I had to acknowledge he was likewise touching, licking, kissing, and holding her.

There came a point in this situationship where I came to grips he was laying down with us both, but this energetic connection, the feeling of him penetrating me just wouldn't leave. This one particular night I was horny, and I wanted him. The girls had already informed me he was not home, and with her living five minutes from me, this was the chance. Our oldest was already living with him, so Sweetpea was staying overnight. Obviously, this allowed me home to sit unbothered. So, I sent the text message, "wyd", and instead of a text back, the telephone started to vibrate. I seen his name, she hoped for delight. "Daddy is coming over". I revealed to him he could drop by knowing he was leaving her. "I am going to fuck the shit out of him", this is what I am saying to myself as I prepare. "What should I wear"? "Red heels, no black ones"? "Pearls or Diamonds"? "Naked or Bra and Panties"? These are the thoughts going through my mind. "This is stupid" should have, but the thought of me giving him this good loving is all I could think while I showered, shaved, and dressed for our night.

My thought was once he gets this matured pussy, it is highly unlikely he is going back to her. I opened myself to him, and I allowed him to molest my soul. We made love, and he went back with her. This enraged my soul. He was whispering in my ear, "I don't know why we getting a divorce". "I still love you". "I miss this good pussy". Ugh, how did I fall into his web?

Although this meet-ups where happening very often, hell it seemed as if we were having more sex pre-divorce than we did when we lived in the same house. These encounters started to occur often, like several times a week, sneak overs, when she's TDY, hell we had sex on Valentine's Day. What I didn't realize was the trap I was putting myself in mentally. I still hadn't laid eyes on the woman, but here I was sleeping with her man. Shit, he wasn't even hers, according to my thoughts, "This dick was still mines".

At last it happened, the other woman was brought into our lives. It was January 2015, a basketball game, our little girl, OUR CHILD, was playing. He comes over and sits with me, takes his position where he dependably sits, directly between my legs. Everything within me was shining and tingling because we had sex not even days before. Not once did I have any signs the fall of Rochelle was going to occur, and this is the night I made the decision for the divorce to go forward. This motherfucker has her at the game, this is a family event, and she is not apart of our team, but she was on his.

She, the other woman, was perched on the visitor's side. You know how you can tell somebody is gazing out at you. I can recall seeing this dark-skinned woman with a dark coat on sitting, and feeling her energy from across the floor. Ladybug, our oldest, comes over as she always does so delightful. She lean over my shoulder, and whispers to me, "Mother, Father's girlfriend is sitting on the visitor's side". Oh, so that's the woman Ladybug was talking with. Now, I see. This woman's daughter was school friends with Ladybug before the connect. Then IT hits me like a ton of brick. The entire time this man has been sitting between my legs, his girlfriend was there, and SHE was the woman I seen Ladybug sitting with. She describes her to me, and as she starts the description, I couldn't focus. The fury started to develop inside my stomach. "How could you bring her to OUR little girls' basketball game"? "Do you have any regard for me, or your little girls"?

After this minute, I don't trust I gave careful consideration to the basketball game with him sitting between my legs, and gazing over the floor at her. The moment to adjust my crown was here. He was playing me, and because of my love for this dick, this energetic connection of lust, I wanted to meet her, see her face to face. Let me see the woman I am sharing my husband with, and let her smell his dick on my breathe. I was going to continue fucking him as long as he said, "On my way"!, not knowing this identity I was about to proclaimed was one being created by him, and I lived it for two years.

From Wife to Side-chick (Identity Theft)

How did I live this life as his wife and a side-chick at the same time? I had lived the life of wife/side-chick for over 15 years and didn't even realize it until the post-divorce side chicking. I was always second to his career and his mother, so the lust planted in my Yoni over 24 years ago has now grew into a stinky pile of "side chick" tendencies. His actions had me in a traffic circle of emotions, and my feelings were on high peak. I didn't know if I was turning left or right. The more love I allowed to pour out from within my heart, he would take every ounce of it, and turn it into more pain and guilt. Everything within me knew what I was doing was wrong. The point of vulnerability came when the energetic lustful feeling shook my soul again. What's going on? Why am I allowing this to happen?

It wasn't until I ended up in a situationship recently, and I am truly meaning recently, where I realized I had enabled the lust from my ex-husband attack my inner being, my soul. Right after I was discharged from the hospital in March 2017, I was ready to replace him. Actually it's only been a few weeks since we stopped sleeping together. So, what's the saying? "To get over one, get under another one". This is bullshit, and I found myself in a situationship of the same shit for almost another year. As I was breaking through my descending fall, I fell into a situationship with a married man. How did I get here? Let me explain how.

As I was genuinely considered the individual who I had become, I realized the identity was given to me years before, and it wasn't mine. The position I took with my ex-husband emptied over into another relationship, even my actions. I was thinking drugs, alcohol, and sex was going to ease the pain. It was the lustful energy, his borrowed energy, left within me which attracted me to this married man. The lustful identity was so deep in my soul it had taken the very essence from me as a woman. The worse happened to me, my identity was stolen. Or did I give up my own identity to emotion, so strong I was blinded?

I thought I was over the pain and guilt of losing my best friend, so I decided to start having some adult time. I love to dance, so I picked a local establishment to have self-care nights. I was going faithfully, meeting new people, receiving compliments, and then I seen HIM. He was a Caramel colored, with these light colored eyes, 6'3" stallion of a body. He drove this green Camaro, so it all fit him well to call him "The Hulk". My "god", was all I could say. He was the perfect man, and my mental stimulation was lit. I prayed for, dreamed about, hell loved this man in my dreams for months, six to be exact. "Ugh, how could I even get close to a man like him"? The Universe asked my prayers, and we finally had the opportunity to meet with one another some months later.

Those side chick tendencies were still there, and the lustful pain and guilt of allowing myself to become my ex-husband's prey, had lead me right into the pasture of another lion. I was eager to forfeit my value, my esteem just to state "I had a man in my bed". The eye opener came with two words, "Side Chick" was spoken to me. Here I am a Domestic Queen about to become a toy for a married man. Sounds so familiar, same song, just a different person playing the drums.

The day, "You are going to make a good side chick", came out the mouth of this married man, I knew Rochelle had taken a detour. I knew right at that point if I enabled this married man to lay between my legs once again, I was going to be the lady I was for the past two years with my ex-husband. Once again, I allowed the control, the manipulation of a narcissistic man's, delicate words controlled my considerations. My spirit was so connected to this position, I was going to enable another man to possess me as his property, his side chick.

It wasn't until this situationship with this married man, that I was able to see the demotion of my value I relinquished being the side chick to my ex-husband. Although I was married for almost 20 years, my ex-husband demonstrated to me a his value of me, a position, he knew lust had taken me, and love would keep me. I was no longer conducting myself as a wife, those significant resources, for example, my notoriety, my respect, what I looked like with my girls, and what I looked like to my friends never at any point truly mattered to me. I heard a invaluable position attached to me. How could I allow all of my value, 19 and a half years, be placed in a position? I was a wife before, and at this moment it hit me. I was comfortable going from wife to side chick, and I was ready to experience this same ID once more.

The Lustful Truth

Being anger was not even the word for the rage I felt inside. Here I am angry and bargaining with myself, accepting the lustful truth, of what I had allowed him to do. Why was I so willing to give myself up to this position? There comes a point in our lives we need to settle on a conscious choice, and take responsibility, During, my time of distress I ended up shouting out to God. I was looking for truth. There was a yearning originating from inside me, and I needed to know more.

What I found was essentially astonishing. During these years of side-sicking with my ex-husband, I was running to the altar seeking deliverance from this lust from "A God". When the time came for me to face this "side chick" identity, I walked away from the four walls. The Spirit separated me, and the greatest transformation began. The discovery, of who God really is lives inside me. It's just plain obvious, this was simply the pull I was feeling. My true self, Phoenix, was going to burst out of my skin. I can remembering entering the doors of this local establishment Sunday after Sunday being told the same, "Keep on praying, God will answer". Truly, HE DID, ONCE I opened, my spiritual eye, my third eye, and accepted the journey to my healing originate from within, the Spirit within, Phoenix, who wrote these prayers to God!

Let's go back to November 2016, where I discovered Phoenix was speaking to Rochelle, my feelings and emotions, and how the separation of the two has me souring today. I was already depressed, although I was telling everyone "I was fine". This part of stage of grief, was a reflection, of the Phoenix I am becoming hiding behind loneliness and side chicking. This is the way my cry began, stage four, reflection and loneliness.

Reflections

November 2, 2016

"Hello. I am so appreciative for YOUR grace and mercy. I know I am not being the best little girl because of one imperfection, my sexual want. Now, I do not understand why I am allowing such a thing to keep me in bondage. We are too close to a breakthrough to allow something as little as this to keep me from walking into YOUR completion". I am asking to remove, kill, and destroy the want to have intercourse and to be licked on. Please forgive me Father for allowing this man to continue to suck the anointing from me".

I was begging for healing. At this point I am months away from my "nervous" breakthrough. I was calling from within for help, and Phoenix was ready to rise. The emotions and feelings of Rochelle just didn't want to let this man go. At this point, I am looking for the Divine One to speak to me in any way and HE did. Once you place intention into the atmosphere the Universe moves, and within days of my request, the Spirit speak.

November 7, 2016

"My daughter and I were on our way to church. We stop by McDonald's for breakfast. The Universe is amazing, and the power of intention is greater. We ordered our food, the cashier says, "Your total is $11:11". I looked at my daughter in awe. We get the receipt and the time was "11:11 a.m". If you know about the number 11, it implies a change in perspective, and I have been asking Spirit to speak. Today is the day! Either I reset my life or die. I was ready to learn, and the Spirit was ready to teach me.

Although I was crying out to the Spirit, I had to realize the some truth. It was these two words mental health or illness which has become a part of me. I realized I was an embarrassment to my ex-husband. In 1996, I was raped in the military, and through coping developed PTSD. I am sitting, thinking about the detrimental effect the mental illness had on our family, but truly the most damage was within me Phoenix was going to reveal the straight truth, and finally I am able to start my journey to healing. The biggest discovery was the Spirit reveals to me, my ex-husband was my assassin.

The reason I refer to him as my assassin is because he wasn't a natural killer of my physical being, but a killer of my spiritual being. The person in whom God had created me to be had taken on the identity of a "side chick" hidden behind a deadly sin of lust, with a touch of "crazy". The true spiritual being within me, was levels above the spiritual and emotional person, in whom he had been groomed. He was a "mama's boy", and in order for him to give me what I needed to go to the next level meant he would have to deny his parents and cleave to who I was becoming so that we could grow together.

The biggest effect was truly on my mental. The emotional, verbal, and spiritual abuse taken over all these years was flooding my emotions. I finally realize my ex-husband was more embarrassed to tell his mom of the illness. It gave the perception I did not want to socialize with them, but in actuality I was grieving for a rape, and grieving from emotional abuse, and he hadn't protected his queen, and didn't have a desire to. I didn't realize until I began to write this chapter there was 10 years of untreated grief coming from within, and wow this was the breakthrough I have waited on. Now it's time for the rising, but first a true falling comes first. The Spirit desired for me to reset, evolve, and transcend through my past, this side chick, stage five, "look back at it".

Look Back At It

I glance back at that individual, the wife to side chick, whose affection ran so deep, she is sincerely joined to this man through her queendom. Wife to side chick, what does this mean. I'm here resetting my mind by detoxing the thought of how could I enable myself to downgraded from a cherishing and minding wife, one who remained behind her man for more than 15 years, but took a position in reverse.

The life, the idea, the identity she adored so much, was being killed by emotional abuse, with unacknowledged grief. I attend an event in Austin, Texas, on March 4, 2017, where I begin to learn more about energy healing and chakra. I was told I was still angry with my ex-husband and I needed to release it. The negative energy was manifesting physically in my body as a heart attack, or CHF, congestive heart failure. The Healer was able to sense this through the warmness of my body in my sacral and root chakra. I know what this means now, but in this moment, I was not trying to hear what the Healer was saying. Angry, no not me.

I ignored what was told to me, and went on with life. Then, the manifestation of the heartbreaking happens. I was leaving a meeting with a young woman I met from the event where I faced my deepest fears. I was examining my decisions and plans of moving forward. For some apparent reason, my feeling and emotions just had to find out the answer to a question brewing from within. Yes, I did it. I called him, and asked him, "What we were doing", since we are still being intimate. His words, entered my soul, and tore every bit of my being out. "I thought we were just having fun", he replies back. What the fuck did he just say, "having fun".

"YOU" have been telling me how much you love me, how YOU couldn't believe we were divorced and how good YOU couldn't believe the loving is. Well, how dumb could I be? To actually believe every word this man has told me. I believed every word he spoke, and it brought much pain. So much, I was willing to kill my physical being to detox, get rid of, his energetic tie to my pain.

I had to accept the fact I allowed my own desires and mindfulness to put me is this position, now this pain has me on the side of the highway crying. An answer I didn't expect, hit me, and I knew I had allowed my life to go far deeper into a pit of love and pain. For two years, two years, post-divorce, you laid between my legs, we snuck around behind our daughters back, our friends, hell your girlfriend's. Now, you're telling me after 15 years of being your wife, the most respect you have for me is to place me in the position of your side chick.

I Found Purpose

The moment when depression and truth are placed before me. I was flooded with rage, disappoint, shame, and the pain was too much. The day of my upward turn came, March 17, four months after writing the entries in my journal. I had an major adjustment, the reset to my life, I found purpose.

I called my oldest daughter to say my goodbyes. I was so over this pain. I had given this man the pure essence of my soul, and he handed it back to me with a label on it. The pain was so overwhelming and driving in front of this 18-wheeler would make it all go around. March 17, 2017, was the beginning of a transformation which amazes me even to this day. Needless to say, I admitted myself into the hospital where I walked in a circle for five days determined to detox myself of this man.

I awaken in Waco at the Veterans Hospital on the psychological well-being ward. I had cried for more than 24 hours. The agony applied for so long of my accepting the manipulation of love from my ex-husband was "grieving" I finally found the strength to gather myself and strolled over to the window. I looked out the window. My thought of being a mom, my girls, and what would be said ran through my head. In regards to all the great things I may have accomplished to this point was now tainted by this breakdown.

I will be known for "being crazy" was going to follow me as their mom. "I knew it." "I knew something wasn't right with her", were words continuously running through my head. I was in this place because of not taking the time to love me and grow mentally and emotionally. I was still more concerned about what individuals would think, oh and my family. Shit what are they going to add to my crazy ass story now. I need to stop this and get myself together.

I was in Waco Veteran's Hospital, in the sunken, dark place of confusion and pain, and the only person able to help me out is me. I'm accepting I have encountered 15 years of passionate, mental, and verbal abuse. I accept I allowed the mishandling of my heart from my ex-husband, as well as, verbal and emotional abuse from his mother came out with every tear. I am standing in this window replaying words spoken to me, incidents between me and the him, the mother's words of disappointment.

There were times I was told, "Why are you not working". "My son is out here working two jobs". "Why are you are home just having babies"? "Why don't you lose some weight"? Ugh, the abusive words and phrases go on and on. I never once spoke anything disrespectful to his mother. Now that I have thought about those moments, if Phoenix was in the light, her ass would have "gotten served the business", but I was so lustful in love with her half-grown son, so I took every blow.

That antisocial young woman, his mother talked me to be; was a hurting woman. I had decided to sell my true identity. Oh, the lifestyle was amazing. Trips around the world at the expense of the military, nice cars, and beautiful homes. Yet deep down inside I was nothing, but a humiliation to him. Defending my condition was not on his priority list of protection. I must say, "Mama Dearest" daughter-in-law with PTSD, oh, and being raped wouldn't make her "glory" topic for his mother's conversation unless it's negative.

Five day later I am ready, to start my rising. I awake the morning of my release determined to go forth in the profound revelation given through the Spirit. The Spirit has revealed God's purpose for me, and the greater part of me wouldn't come forth until I let go of my former life, and this psychological break gave me the courage to accept the role I played in the facade, and prepare for Phoenix to come forth.

The months following I poured into myself through the healing practices of Reiki. I grew in strength of who I was becoming spiritually and allowed reconstruction to begin. I was working through the pain to find my purpose, stage five. I was gaining the power to rise above this facade of a life I had grew to lustful love. The day I walked out the hospital, Rochelle was impregnated with Phoenix, and nine months she would make her debut.

The Spirit attuned me to a power of healing from within. I studied myself, separated myself, cried by myself, but most of all I accepted my true self. I cannot be angry at my ex-husband for not being able to love at the level I was growing. He would always tell me even when we were married, "he didn't know me", and now I over stand why. Rochelle was there giving her all to this life she was living to live for the lustful love of a man, who later who only value her from his selfish ways.

Phoenix was making herself known, and on November 11th, 2017, I finally decided to do it. I began to rebrand myself in rebirthing as Phoenix J Ma'ri., the ending to all of the stage before, and beginning with hope and acceptance. The willings to accepting my healing opened my life to the spirit within me, which forced me to stage of from grief to grind.

From Grief to Grind

November 11th, 2017, is my PHEE (Freedom) birthday. If you can recall me speaking earlier, of how the Spirit spoke clearly to me on November 11, 2016. The breakdown was truly the breakthrough to Phoenix. After walking in a circle for five days the Spirit confirmed my yearning to learn more was correct, and now with Reiki, I am living life free of the brokenness and healing from years of emotional, verbal, and spiritual abuse .

My spiritual being, mind, body, and soul has now taken on the perceptive of the Divine One. I am able to see the world clearly, and accept those things I cannot change. Meditation is a very big part of my new life, and this truly has assisted in me growing from suicidal to peace. There was this idea of me living life only with my ex-husband, living the life we pillowed talked about was not the life God purposed for me.

I didn't work for 20 years, so starting a business was the only way to overcome the fear of starting again without a man; and I did it. I "looked back at it", my past, as it refers to my path. The place, the broken, sunken area that I had allowed myself to fall into is now filled with the love of Spirit.

The Divine Spirit revealed my true purpose, and I am walking it out in fire. I am a Reiki Practitioner, where I assist women in rebirthing a victorious Y.O.U. (Your Own Uniqueness) , to become a better version of yourself, and Chakra Healer. This path has attuned my inner being to LOVE Rochelle's emotions and feeling, her true dedication, loyalty, and most of all her strength. I rejoice in my new living as a Reiki Practitioner, a Transformation Life Coach, Advocate for Domestic Violence, and so much more to come.

Not long after my final breakdown, the breakthroughs began, and I was able to adjust my crown, not in shock or denial, but empowered and evolved. Not as my ex-husband's side chick or anyone else's, but as a grinding goddess. I am accepting MY upward turn, MY God purposed life.

He granted me the opportunity months after my breakdown, on September 16, 2017 to share my story. I was the Keynote Speaker at the First Annual Central Texas Veterans Health Care System, "Hats and Heels Empowerment Celebration". I walked into the clinic for a checkup, and walked out the keynote speaker. I shared my story with the administration for the Women's Clinic, and the doors continue to open. My gratitude to the position God has given me is so much greater than being a side chick. I truly had to accept the past me was not the real me. She was a woman willing to sell her life and dignity for a love only the Divine One could give. The Spirit is growing within me daily, and the energetic spirit, filled with love as Phoenix J Ma'ri will continue to blaze the world with truth, wisdom, and understanding so women can have a true meaning when it comes to self-care, self-love, and self-fishiness.

CHAPTER FIVE

My Pride And Joy Is Gone

To understand my grief, you had to understand what type of person my son was.
I received a call from John's kindergarten teacher saying that he was hyper and disruptive to the class. She wanted him tested for ADHD. My immediate response was John does not have ADHD; he is merely bored in your class. A couple weeks went by and I got another call, this one quite different.
"Mrs. Davis, we tested John and it appears that he is beyond the kindergarten level in his knowledge." John was able to spell and write his name, he knew and recognized the entire alphabet as well as his numbers to 100. He was actually starting on the second grade reading level. John was an outstanding student. He was well advanced in his years and this continued through elementary school. He was actually recognized by his daycare for outstanding achievement and received his first $50 savings bond at the ripe young age of 7 years old. I made sure he was involved in sports at a young age as well. He played T-ball, basketball, football and soccer while I was stationed in Germany and Missouri.

We were a military family so traveling and moving to different schools happened often. When John reached junior high school, he was placed in honors classes and maintained a 4.0 grade point average through high school to graduation. While in 9th grade, at Tomlinson Junior High School, he received the highest honor given by the school. He was crowned T-Day King. He was nominated by the teaching staff based on academic and sports excellence. The students voted and crowned him king among 10 young men nominated. He excelled in football and basketball. He was on a traveling basketball team as well, playing games throughout Oklahoma and Texas. John started his sophomore year off at Kentridge High School in Seattle, Washington and played on the football and basketball teams there. Later that school year he moved to Cocoa Beach, Florida and played on the Cocoa Beach High School football team. My baby shined. I knew from the moment I found out God had given him his gift he was a force to be reckoned with.

    He was selected to the All Space Coast Conference Team in 2002 and 2003. He was selected to play in the Brevard County All-Star football game in 2003 and was a key player on the 2004 Cocoa Beach State Basketball Team and graduated that year with honors. Watching my young man grow into his own. A mother's dream and the world better watch out because John is about to rule the world. As spectacular as John is why play one sport. He also ran track (the high jump and hurdles) and played basketball. While doing that he injured his knee. Not enough to prevent him from playing. What a relief. My pride and joy still needed surgery. As always we knew that only meant more greatness.

    The moment most parents have been waiting for. Graduation time! My pure emotions to over me knowing that my pride and joy will be Graduating with honors. A mother's smile and nervousness. As my John received a full academic scholarship to several colleges but chose to attend the University of Florida (UF). Yes, the boy that was jumping up and down in class. Yes, my gifted child got a full ride to one of the best colleges in the nation. I am so proud of him! As a young man growing into his own John was a determined young man and never allowed anyone or anything to hold him back. What John didn't know was he inspired me and still does daily. John ended up having his surgery. After reconstruction surgery on his knee, he walked onto the Florida Gators football team. The determination of playing the game that brought him so much joy. He proved that he was not going to be held down nor held back and worked hard to obtain a full football scholarship from the University of Florida as well and was a member of the 2006 and 2008 National Championship Teams.
Wow to hear John's voice when he realized that God's gift will be seen on national T.V. Better yet the feeling of happiness I got hearing his voice. Thank you God for giving me John.

After graduating in 2009 from UF, things got real. As his mother this is where it gets hurtful and real for me too. John graduation was a joy to see but several of his friends and college teammates went on to play in the National Football League (NFL). Deep down I knew the injuries plagued him while in college, he had several injuries and surgeries that did not afford him the opportunity to be drafted by the NFL. It's hard to described a mother's pain after hearing and seeing her son's pain. His dream was over. The degree he obtained didn't mean much if he wasn't touching that ball.

Upon his graduation, he returned to Seattle, where his father resided. This was not ideal for John at all. But as a man you do what you have to do. He worked as a manager of Ezell's Chicken at the Lake City location. The dream comes in so many different forms. He had the opportunity to play football in the state of Washington for both the Kent Predators Indoor Football team and the South King County Colts Semi-Pro team. Graduated and he can still touch the ball. Being a military family is tough. The moves and deployments can take a toll on you. In 2001, I was in the Army and was on orders to Korea for one year. This was the start of his sophomore year and the first year of high school. I allowed John and his two younger brothers to stay with their father while on assignment to Korea. This was the start of his sophomore year and the first year attending high school. So much happened in that short year. My grandmother became gravely ill and passed away. 30 days later, my sister's house was deliberately set on fire and she lost her two youngest daughters that day. It had also been the longest the children and I had been separated in about 10 years. Little did I know that this was the start of his depression and changed the joy that he displayed. John sometimes called and expressed things the average person wouldn't consider a problem. Not hitting 5 3-points shots in a basketball game or getting a B on a paper. Then the issues became bigger and more serious. They were directed towards how his father would talk down to him about the things he did or didn't do to his satisfaction. When John graduated from college, he decided to move back to the Seattle, Washington area and live with his father. The calls became more intense and there were a lot of middle of the night calls where he was quite upset and crying. He mostly talked about how disappointed his father was with him. He once said his father told him that he had a bullshit job. John felt that he was always belittled by his father. As a mother what do you do when you hear you precious gift from God hurting.

The Bible is clear in how parents should handle our precious children. God said it twice, once in Colossians and once in Ephesians. Fathers, provoke not your children to anger, lest they be discouraged (Col 3:21); and, yes father, provoke not your children to wrath (Eph 6:4). With it being said more than once, it must have been important that we love and support our children and not discourage them. Positive affirmations are so very important to a child's, even an adult's, development.

On the morning of 5 August 2010, I received a call from John. I could tell he was upset but didn't understand the magnitude of his pain during the call. He asked me if I was disappointed in him. I tried to reassure him that I was proud of him. The pain I felt hearing John. I was beyond proud. He graduated high school with honors, he graduated from college, he didn't have any children yet, and he was working. He was only 24 years old. He had made some mistakes, like we all had, but he had his whole life in front of him. The things we prepare our kids for and they accomplish them should be enough right?

I guess hearing these words weren't enough to reverse the damage and negativity that-plagued him since going to live with his father. Shortly after that conversation, John took his own life by falling from the fourth floor of a building in front of many witnesses. My pride and joy left me. Depression, negative talk, life, expectations, and pain took over. Now here we are.

My pride and joy John was a very outgoing young man that was well liked by all. He had an infectious smile that will forever be ingrained in the hearts and minds of the people he encountered. Let me tell ya'll about this smile John had. Pearly white teeth and charming. John's whole being lite up a room. He apparently was living two lives though. No one knew the true him inside. He always appeared to be having the best of times with his friends. This is what I imagined was going through his head:

"Everyone follows me on social media sites and text me back and forth, but I have no one to talk to or walk with. I am invited to all the events and parties, but still I am lonely. I have all the friends in the world but still feel like no one really knows me." He was going through pain but never showed that side of himself. Was he hiding his true self from us or was it something we never asked him about. He masked his sadness with what looked like the ideal lifestyle. His outward appearance was so happy but he was struggling with depression and anxiety on the inside. John drank to drown his pain but his pain learned how to swim. He tried to bury his fears but they began to fly and circle his head. He was sick of crying, tired of trying, smiling but yet dying. Isn't it amazing how we can think we know someone and still don't know them at all?

After hearing the news of his death, I absolutely felt the life being sucked right out of me. He could not take the feeling of resentment and disappointment from his dad. My pride and joy was gone. The pain of losing a child is indescribable. There are no words to explain the feeling of knowing your firstborn is no longer living. We took a family trip and drove across country a couple of months before. I was in El Paso, Texas at the time. I drove my car to Dallas and picked up a rental van. Then, I drove that rental to Lawton, Oklahoma to pick up Ronnell and Jeremiah, their children's mother, and my grandchildren. We drove to St. Louis, Missouri and picked John up from the airport. We had the whole plan mapped out. We drove to Columbus and Youngstown, Ohio to gather with family. We reconnected with some and met others. It was such a joyous time. Who knew that would be the last time any of us would see him again.

I was at work on that tragic day when I received the phone call. All I could do was drop to the floor searching for answers. Answers I will never find. I didn't want to talk to anyone. I didn't want to eat or sleep. I just wanted to know why. The last thing I wanted was anyone to say to me was they understood. How could anyone understand the relationship I had with my children? How can anyone possibly know the pain and emptiness this left me? I was supposed to protect him. He kept reaching out for help, and the signs were there. Was I too close to the situation? Or, was I being optimistic that things would change? Surely, no one knew how I felt. How do you recover from something like that? First, you cry a lot then cry some more. I jumped right to what if and only if scenarios that could have saved him. After that I felt like I couldn't go on, and I would never be the same. Even to this day, I always wonder why it happened and what could've been different.

After the shock dissipated just a little, I had to deal with burying my beloved son. My sister, Diane was my rock through the entire process. She was my strength and my shield. I pray that I was the same to her eight years prior when we lost my nieces. Surely, if anyone could imagine some of the pain I was experiencing it was her. I couldn't do anything for myself, so trying to do anything to prepare for a funeral was beyond anything I could comprehend at that time. Diane contacted our aunt, who was a funeral director. Together they contacted the coroner in Seattle to release the body to only L.E. Black Funeral Home in Youngstown, Ohio. Of course this was the right thing to do since that is where his dad and I were from. Also, this was where the majority of our families were. Well, that was met with great opposition from his dad. Even John's only other aunt had something negative to say (like I didn't have enough to worry about). Now, I had people with all these opinions trying to tell me what to do. How could anyone have the audacity to tell me what to do with my son's remains or where to bury him?

I carried him for nine months. I took care of him and nurtured him. He only went to stay with his father because I was trying to be nice, and I had to go overseas for that year. By that time, I had raised him the best way I knew how. His father didn't even want me to have him. He told me to get an abortion. So I think I did a darn good job if I say so myself. I tried to do my best to raise my kids to the best of my ability. I didn't have a great example to follow. My parents did not support me like they should have. I stayed most of my childhood at my grandma's house with my cousins while our parents partied or did whatever they were doing. I did not look up once and see them in the stands during one of the football games, basketball games, or track meets. See being a cheerleader and running track was my passion. Although my dad provided the money to do these things, there was zero emotional support. This is something I needed. I needed their emotional support. I needed to know they had my back and wanted to see me flourish in my passions. Still to this very day in 2018, I don't feel the emotional support from my parents. My love language is "Quality Time." I guess you have to spend time with me to know that. I don't need stuff. You don't have to buy me material things because that does not tell me you love me. Buying material things tell me that you feel you have an obligation to do something for me. God did not give you children, so that you have an obligation to raise them. He commanded that you nurture and raise children in admonition of the Lord. Start children off in the way they should go, and even when they are old, they will not turn from it is something I truly believe.

  Everything I learned about being a mother and being there for my children, I had to learn on my own. School events, I was there. Sporting events, I was there. Sometimes running from one arena to another, but I was there. I never received that from my own mother. The only thing that I learned from her was to never have anything of my own and to always depend on someone else to take care of me. I wanted to be better and do better by my own. I so didn't want to be anything like her. This is what being nice got me. Because I was having a hard time dealing with the situation of losing my eldest child to a senseless death and people, Diane handled all my calls. John's father told Diane, "This is not a conversation that we should be having. I need to talk to your sister." Diane is not a person you want to have opposition with.

  She politely told him "I am my sister, we are one! I am her mouthpiece while she can't speak." John's Father told us that John didn't like Youngstown, and he don't want to be buried there. Now, where that came from I had no idea. We had a blast there two months prior and John didn't want to leave. Family was everything to us and we loved being around family. His father told me that he would get buddy passes for me to fly to

Washington to have his funeral there. So, I was not to have his funeral near our families but in some strange town I visited once. Man, I knew he was crazy. This man even called my father and told him I was being unreasonable. Boy, was that a mistake. If you know my father, you will not call him and talk negatively about me or my siblings. He can talk about us all he wants, but nobody else is going to talk about us. I am the oldest child and John was the oldest grandchild. Now you know how that conversation went. Bet, he won't call my father anymore and talk about his daughter.

Because John was so well liked by everyone he encountered, Bishop Harris, from Free Gospel Church in Lawton, Oklahoma loaded up a church van with his family and some of the church members and drove to Ohio to preside over his funeral. This was a testament to what type of character John possessed. Not every day you have people drop what they are doing, drive over 1,100 miles to support you even in death. Bishop Harris and many others met John when he was just 13 years old and followed him through junior high, high school, and college. They supported him in all of his achievements. They showed up at his football and basketball games. They were present when he won his awards and accolades. He was so loved and admired. The funeral home was overflowing with people showing their love and support for him. So many people who knew John made sacrifices to be there for his home-going services. Even 4 of John's friends he met at college made the trip from different parts of Florida to be there for the services. Because of previous commitments, like training camp with the NFL, his college roommate wasn't able to attend. So my question was, why couldn't John's father take those same buddy passes for the airline and come to his own son's funeral? Why didn't he take one of those buddy passes and give to his sister, John's aunt, the one who wanted to tell me that I was wrong for bringing his body to Youngstown to bury him there? Why didn't she show up to his funeral? It wasn't like they didn't have a place to stay; their father still lives there to this day. On the other hand, I had a large family to be concerned with. It wasn't feasible for us to have the funeral anywhere else. The least amount of sacrifices was on the paternal side of the family. They should have been there. Even my ex-husband, the man who helped me raise John, found a way to make it to the funeral.

It's so funny how God convicts the heart of people though. John's aunt called me almost eight years later to apologize. I was appreciative that she called and tried to make it right, but I simply thought 'sister you are too late with that apology'. I wasn't moved at that moment at all. My number had not changed one digit since she called me; not to offer condolences but to scold me on my decisions to do what I wanted with the child I carried and had to make the decision to give life to, even if I had it do it solo. alone. If others that were not a part of the immediate family could make time, find a way, and sacrifice a little, why couldn't the people who should have been there if no one else was there? I'm still bitter about that.

The ignorance continued. Instead of calling someone in my family to get the correct names of John's immediate family members (for example my father's last name, my mother's last name, my sister's first name and brother's last name), all of these were printed up wrong in the obituary that was produced in Seattle, Washington for his memorial service there. He didn't have to talk to me. He could've called someone, anyone, to find out the information. Little things like that matter and attest to the things John had to endure from his father, even in death. At this point, not only was I grieving because I lost my first born, but I was grieving because of ignorance of people. John was about 6'3 and had very broad shoulders, and an average size coffin was not going to hold him unless I wanted him to look like a stuffed potato. Therefore, I needed to get a bigger coffin, which was more money. Limos, flowers, burial plot, headstone, and funeral services all cost a lot of money. The unexpected death of a child cost lots of money. No one on the paternal side of the family had the decency to ask me how much I needed for the services. Actually, it was stated to me that John's grandmother's funeral cost about $5000. Well, in the year 2010, I wasn't able to get anything close to $5000, try doubling that after receiving discounts because we were family. Needless to say, I didn't get much help from his dad to give this child a proper burial. Lord

let me tell you, a mother will do what she can for her children. If that meant I had to call and get an increase to the credit limit of my credit card, my baby wasn't going to have just a simple little burial. I was going to make the best of this tragic situation as possible.
After John's death, I learned a lot about suicide. I now had a personal experience with it. I can't tell you the number of times I thought about committing suicide myself. There are so many days I would like to end it all. All the pain, all the agony, so many disappointments, is too much for a mother, a sister, a daughter, or a friend to handle. Because I genuinely cared about others and cared what others thought of me, it got discouraging at times. I kept telling the psychiatrist, I have thoughts but could not and would not act on them because I knew the devastation it would leave for the surviving family members.

  People think that depression is sadness. People think that depresses crying. They think that depression is being quiet. Depress is when you smile but want to cry. It's when you talk but want to be quiet. It's when you pretend that you're happy when in actuality you are at your lowest. Depression is not always obvious. You don't know how stressful it is to explain what's going on in your head when you don't even under it yourself. A person who is suicidal needs to know you care. Listen to him or her. Ask questions. Help the person to discuss his or her feelings. Show that you take the person's feelings serious and want to help. Explain that with help and support he or she can recover. It's ok to FaceTime, but make sure to spend some quality face to face time. Suggest sources of help. Stay close until professional help is available. Don't try to shock or challenge. Don't analyze the person's motives. Don't argue or try to reason. Say something to encourage positive action or improve the home environment. If the home life is a problem, suggest a way to improve it such as getting counseling or family therapy. People with depression often become inactive and grow more depressed and withdrawn. Help the person balance work and recreation in his or her daily schedule. Even a temporary change of scene can make a big difference. This is a chance to gain a new outlook on the situation. Exercise can help the person feel better. It is good to get 30 minutes or more moderate physical activity on most days, prayerfully, all days of the week. Suggest solutions to the problem. Let the person know that no problem it is too big to solve. Suggest that he or she talk about it. Holding back feelings won't solve anything. If the problem involves other people, encourage the person to work it out with them. Try to change the situation. Help the person find a positive way to resolve a stressful situation. Learn to relax. Hobbies, sports, and relaxation techniques such as deep breathing can help the person handle stress more effectively. Your health is important, but you can't do it alone. Encourage the person to get professional help. When people don't post on social media for a few days, we ask if they're ok. When someone posts every day, we assume they are fine. Tell people you love them. Be a trustworthy friend. Ensure you are letting people know they matter. Robin Williams said, before he committed suicide, "I used to think the worst thing in life was to end up alone. It's not! The worst thing in life is to end up with people who make you feel alone." And if you are thinking about suicide ask for help. Let others know. Share your feelings with someone such as a relative, friend, healthcare provider, teacher, counselor, or religious leader. Call the suicide hotline. The national hotline network is 1-800-suicide. In an emergency, call 911 or a local medical emergency number. Talk to a mental health professional. They are trying to help people who are thinking about suicide. Ask a relative or friend to stay with you, if it is not possible go to a nearest healthcare facility. Avoid all alcohol and other drugs. They can make it hard for you to think clearly.

   Grief is a painful experience, but the pain does subside. Because everyone experiences loss or change at some time in life, understanding grief can help you get help you -face the reality and deal with feelings of fear, loneliness, despair and helplessness. Recover and grow to be a stronger person. Accepting your loss can help you live a happy, full life again. Grief is part of the healing process. Grieving people share certain feelings.

Shock and Denial: Your first reaction may be to deny your loss or to feel emotionally numb. Eventually, you'll be able to face the reality of your loss.

Anger: your loss may seem unfair. You may feel angry with yourself and others for not preventing the loss. But you can work through your anger.

Guilt: It is not unusual to blame yourself for something you did or didn't do prior to your loss. Remember, you are only human. There are events you just can't control or undo.

Depression: You may feel drained and unable to perform basic, routine tasks. Eventually, you will become involved in life again.

Loneliness: Increased responsibilities and changes in your life can make you feel lonely and afraid. As you meet new challenges and develop new friendships, these feelings will fade.

Acceptance: You will reach a stage where you can accept your loss and look to your future with hope.

No matter how difficult life may get, you can pull through! Living with a loss means you must take care of your emotional needs by expressing your feelings. Holding painful feelings inside can create more problems. Accept help. Friends and family can make difficult moments easier. For many people, participation in and support from a spiritual community can be a great comfort. I asked for help. Relatives and friends want to help, but I often don't know what to do. Professional help is also available if feelings of despair and worthlessness persist. Be kind to yourself. Some days will be more difficult than others, but you will recover. Do activities you enjoy, such as taking a walk or going to a movie or reading. Get plenty of rest. You'll have more energy to handle problems and get involved in activities. Stay healthy. Eat a variety of foods and exercise regularly. Avoid alcohol, sedatives, and other potentially harmful substances. Be alert for problems. If you don't seem to feel better over time, it may not be due to just grief. Poor sleep, weight loss, and low energy may be signs of depression, which is a treatable condition.

Tears are not a sign of weakness. Tears are a natural way to release intense feelings. There is no shame in showing how you feel. Children should not be sheltered from grief. Children need to grieve. Tell them about the loss in an honest loving way. It is best to discuss loss with a grieving person. Grieving people are grateful for friends who share memories and talk about the pain created by the loss. An end to grief does not mean an end to the caring about a loved one. Love last beyond grief through a commitment to live life fully.

At the release of this book it would have been the eighth year anniversary of John's death. Eight is the number of new beginnings. Life has to go on. Not only did I have to survive, I now have two sons who have lost their older brother and have challenges of their own on top of dealing with the loss of someone they looked up to. After the funeral I wondered: now what? How do I move on? Where do I go from here? There was no way I would ever be the same. The first sermon I heard after the death of my son that I wrote down and actually heard was "Increasing Your Believing Capacity." The first thing I was to do was 'Decide To Believe'. Some of my beliefs I held after conscious deliberation. Other beliefs just seem to have been there forever, as a natural part of life. And sometimes, beliefs seem to take hold of me almost against my will. But, how do I strike the balance? Faith positions (fighting my faith), whether positive or negative (it is God, me and my flesh), can take of these forms. First let me say that there are careful, slow, and rational conversions and losses of faith; there are sudden moments of enlightenment, and for some people faith, or lack of it, is entirely taken for granted. I had to trust and believe in The Father. I had to not lean on my own understanding. I had to believe my son was not being tormented by naysayers, but he was at peace. I had to believe that God knew he was burdened and heavy laden and He gave rest to John's weary soul even if I thought I was being robbed of this life. I had to remind myself of this: Dorsetta, you have to trust and believe that God makes no mistakes!

  Secondly, 'Believe The Promises Of Jesus.' Jesus promised that He would not leave us or forsake us. We are the head and not the tail. Jeremiah 29:11 says, 'For I know the plans

I have for you,' declares the Lord, 'plans to prosper you and not to harm you, plans to give you hope and a future.' Psalms 23:4 tells me 'Even though I walk through the darkest valley, I will fear no evil, for you are with me; your rod and your staff, they comfort me.' Isaiah 40:29 ensures me that 'He gives strength to the weary and increases the power of the weak. I knew that if I patiently endure, I'll receive the promises.' From first to last, scriptures in the Bible are filled with God's promises to us. And it's only the promises of God that call forth our faith, fill us with hope and love, and nourish courage in us to live in the world, but not of the world. Therefore, it's imperative that I endeavor to believe God's promises to me. According to Everett E. Storms there are 7959 promises in Scripture made by God. If we use one promise each day it will take us 22 years to use each of the promises once. Caleb lived 40 years on one promise. How many years can we live on 7959 promises?

Third thing is be 'Single-Minded.' What do you mean I have to focus on one thing at a time? There were so many thoughts going through my head. So many questions I needed answers to. God was saying be still and know that I am God. I needed to let go and let God. He is sovereign in my life and only He could direct my path. II Corinthians 10:5-6 gave me a very important directive. It tells me to 'take every thought captive' and to deal with the thoughts that are not of faith. God knows that taking every thought captive is critical because my thoughts are the first to be triggered in the chain-reaction of my soul. In other words, my thoughts stir up my emotions; my emotions then influence my choices; and, my choices are what produce my life. Thus, whatever controls my thinking will ultimately be what controls my life.

The fourth lesson was to 'Be Unwavering In Pursuit Of My Goals.' Many people consistently complain about not getting something; about not achieving their goals; and about all the obstacles and problems that make their life "oh so difficult". These people would immediately quit complaining the moment they realized that: we don't get what we want; we only get what we are 100% committed to. In other words, unless I am fully committed to something, I don't have a hope in the world of bringing my desires into reality. However, it is important that I take ownership of this vision. Therefore, this vision must be of my creation and not based on someone else's idea. I must own it, and I must take full responsibility for bringing this vision into reality. That is the only way I will ever fully commit to this path. It means that I trust God with my life more than I trust myself. It means that I trust His timing even when I'm running out of patience. It means that I trust His decisions even if I don't like them. It means that I will love Him with all my heart even if I don't understand Him. It means that even when I question Him, I still believe in Him. Even when I'm tired from everything He's been throwing my way, I can sleep with my mind at ease because I know He knows what He's doing. It means that I accept what He's written for me even if I'm dying to change it. It means that instead of fighting with Him, I fight for Him. It means that instead of complaining to Him, I thank Him.

The fifth thing I was supposed to do was 'Live My Life With A Sense of Destiny.' I was supposed to have a vision and commit to excellence. Now God, you know my business partner just died. He had all the plans, and he had the licenses for the business. He had the vision on how to pursue this adventure. This business is something me and John was going to do together and John was no longer here. Knowing that I had recently sent John all the material for the business, I figured I would contact his father so he could send them to me. Of course, he couldn't or wouldn't find them. So what now?

When you are living out your purpose in life, you are living your personal meaning of destiny. When you are aligned with your destiny, your life is joyful, delightful, exciting, and fulfilling. Destiny is life's journey. I must constantly ask myself, "What is my purpose?" Passions change and morph over time as I came to know and understand myself more deeply. As I followed my passions, I found myself drawn irresistibly onward until one day I woke up and found I was living a passionate life, filled with a sense of destiny. My destiny is a very personal path, and no one can walk it for me or tell me where to go. No one can tell me how to change my life in order to live out my meaning of destiny. It is up to me to discover my passions and live what I truly love to do, but once this happens my life will be irresistibly pulled in directions I have not ever imagined. T.D. Jakes said "Everything you've gone through is preparation for what's about to happen in your life. The LORD has already given you a word, MOVE!" When we "move," we bring about the growth we desire. Tragedy hasn't stopped me, heartbreak didn't defeat me, and failure does not define me. I had to use this hard-earned wisdom to grasp my purpose and shape my future.

I had to recognize the gifts God had given me. I had been dealt some cards in my life. These included things I couldn't control - my parents or my kids, my nationality, my race, or my language. They also include my SHAPE - my spiritual gifts, my heart, my abilities, my personality and my experiences. They're all the things that make me uniquely me.

God has given me gifts for a purpose. I have a responsibility to be a good steward of these gifts, not for selfish use, but for the good of others. The gifts aren't for my benefit. God gave them to me for the benefit of other people. I have to know my purpose. I have to stay encouraged until that purpose is fulfilled. It may take a long time for God's will in my life to come to pass because he is shaping and molding me every day. I just need to stay the course. I can't get discouraged not knowing how to reach that destiny or seeing it in the near future. I can't lose sight of my purpose. I must keep the vision of the end goal before me. Nobody but me can stop my destiny!

CHAPTER SIX
Release Grief Obtain Love

Dick pics and I'm smiling, I'm cheesing, and I'm excited as hell! All the words carrying orgasmic powers of fantasy in action as he spoke. I felt my nature moisten and my imagination started to flow. I was being devoured on the beach with only my desires and passions being catered to. I pictured the lake, the waterfall sounds and views, and dinner on the rocks. My mind was creating visions and thoughts I thought were dead in me. I was momentarily experiencing myself pre-anguish, pre-pain, pre-unhappiness, and pre-grief. I was fully aware and open to new possibilities, ones I didn't see before. When grief hits, you have no idea the emotional, physical, and mental changes it will make within.

"Wait a mutha effin minute, you mean to tell me I can get her back"? I was of course talking to myself. I awakened, and with that passion and energy, I moved forward to get that old thang back! I am yet at another crossroad of choosing IT over ME. Sitting here wondering how I lost a part of myself, my imagination and lust for love. I once lost myself, and I can't afford to have that happen again. I allowed my experiences to dictate who I became. Let's go back so you can get a better glimpse of it all.

I wonder sometimes am I the only one that feels this way. Society tells us how to think and what we should look like, all the while damaging the very essence of what it is to be human and unique. As a woman being told that you are the problem when someone hurts you is damaging. Or being told you are required to look like this, speak like this, or act like that!
How does one exist in a bipolar double standard world? Seriously, am I the only one? We are now so connected, we know we are being lied to, we know that we have been sacrificed, undermined, underappreciated, devalued, underserved, and unprotected, but we still sit in silence. We try to keep the high regard of others, but never really having that same high regard for

ourselves. We also don't require this regard from others. Is this who we are and why we are here and what we stand for? We are put in competition when none exists. We are divided in our unity due to inherited shame, denial, and false acceptance that will never be obtained. We are continuing the behavior that further dismantles and divides us….why? I grieve over our power that we allow to be wasted; I grieve the time that we waste on others but won't give to ourselves; I grieve the unity in our families; I grieve for my grandma encountered so much more and received so much less. So in grieving parts of me, I am grieving so many other things simultaneously. Am I the only one that feels this way?

    I lived freely from what I can remember as a child. I guess you could say I was a dreamer, not a realist. I was the type of girl that if I liked you I told you, I was not fearful of being turned down or scared of rejection. I had a particular group of friends that hold tough even today! I believe I was always a people person and open to almost anything. I wouldn't say I was a thrill seeker, but I had no problem doing anything I wanted to do. I was good about calculating the outcomes of a situation to determine if it was something I wanted to do. I've never been a fighter or the jealous type. I tried my best to be respectful and friendly to people. I have lived a lifetime of living as me but living for others. Let me explain. My youngest memory was running around and telling my siblings what to do. I was the head of the household so my demeanor became that. I was in charge, I was responsible, and I was the order that was put in place to keep the function of it all in the absence of my parents. I had my siblings, cousins, and friends watching me, waiting for me to lead, waiting for me to be this person they knew I was and would be. I was the big sister, the one everyone watched, followed, judged, and mimicked. I was so many things but not always myself. Shit, I never really knew myself, just the self I created based on the perceptions and guidance of others for me. Being responsible, being in charge, and being bossy so early gave me a good start on life, especially as I sit now telling mutha effas what I'm gonna do! (Laughing) But, I entered into this world and slowly adjusted to becoming a product of my environment.

Well, that's how I remember myself, before I allowed my life experiences to shape my life and dictate my outcome. I eventually became all the things that I was not. So many times I have lost something, I have cried, I have moved on in pain and never actually processed the grief. Being told to "get over it" or "it happens to everyone" or even "it could be worse" pushed me to a point of helplessness. I mean if there is no relief, no logical way of processing grief, we will forever grieve. Who would want to live this way if all that existed were unnecessary griefs that happened for a reason and could not be controlled? For me, this was something that became unbearable as I continued living. Always seeing the dismay in all things and never the abundance, I started to detach from life, but this didn't happen until much later when I was assaulted. I felt I had lost complete control of ANY and EVERY thing due to the invasion of my privacy. So there I was in a shell, grieving, and had no idea how to handle grief properly. I turned on myself, still excelling to the outside but fighting with myself inside for the will to be able to see greater than my life experiences.

Throughout my life I saw pain, I saw hurt, I saw people experience the good and not so good things in life. I never saw anyone process these things. I never saw the family conversations about how to heal from ailments of life. I saw people adapt and live through the experiences, pushing past them seemed to be the way to move forward from what I experienced. Now looking back, I can only imagine how those before us were hindered due to not knowing how to process grief in a healthy way. Even now, I know people push through as they downplay the significance of what seem to be insignificant events. I couldn't push past, I tried, but over and over after my assault, I pretended and moved forward as if everything was ok. I was existing as Myesha, but she wasn't present anymore. Grief had shut her down and shut down any possibility of greatness down right along with her. What does this look like? For me, it looked like complacency, drinking, seclusion, internally exceeding but meeting the bare minimum. I was not who I was prior to grief, and I spent years trying to get back to the pre-grief me.

Anguish, unhappiness, heartache, pain, misery, and sorrow are just some of the words that describe grief. We all have grieved in some way, shape, or form; yet, how we dealt with it, and how we currently deal with it is what separates us. I had to grieve myself; yes, I had to grieve the Myesha that was or could have been or should have been (according to others). I lost her when I was 19 from my memory. Her smile, her enthusiasm, and her happiness in life was gone. She was my best friend, and I had lost her. I only had vague memories of her and couldn't even relate to the happiness she once held inside her. She was a boss by nature; she was independent, relatable, friendly, and super funny. The me I remembered and the me I lost, I so want to have her back exactly as she was; but that seems to only be an imaginary venture that never comes to fruition. The most interesting part about losing yourself is thinking you are there the whole time and in fact are not lost.

Grief for me is not a process that is without heavy sacrifice and energy, and I value my growth. Grief processing for me is extremely exhausting, even all these years later. The fact that I have to mourn over and over in order to heal so many things is exhausting within itself. I am so honored by the people that are sharing and healing throughout the world on so many levels. I share because I understand it is bigger than me. Even writing this work is very tiring; having to reprocess, envision, and feel what you felt at that time in reliving these moments is draining. I have shared my story over and over and really while it does help, I spend a lot of time mourning and grieving because I am living this experience literally. During the journaling for this book, I contemplated not sharing because I was at that very moment processing a whole other type of grief. As I share, I heal and healing isn't always comfortable but always worth it. I often am alone with my feelings and emotions so that makes it harder to continuously open up, but still I do.

When I processed that I encountered a man that decided to take what he wanted from me with no regard of me, initially I lost myself. It was like being in my body, but my spirit was gone. I went through the pain of accusing the man, filing a report, enduring medical examinations. I pushed through the system to carry on with my life. I was basically living as a shell of myself, a soft shell at that. I stopped hanging out, I was shunned by female peers, and out casted. I tried my best to constantly protect my environment by only going to places that were safe. My life was nothing as I wanted it to be, but everything outside of me was telling me that this was now how it had to be. Grief had taken over my life, and I was there for the ride.

    Finding out that I was pregnant was a shock, not because I wasn't having sex (for you smart ones out there); it was because I had been on birth control for 14 years. I went from thinking it was a late period, to clots, to a miscarriage in about 4 days. I didn't even have time to process. I thought I was going to have another baby, not planned, nothing like I wanted, but I was ok with it. I knew whatever was happening was going to happen…and then it didn't. I cried, eyes were puffy, and I started to grieve the life that could have been. I wasn't far along nor did I build a bond, but the connection was still a piece of me. A piece of me that I will never get to see, it was pretty tough for me, but I processed through it and that's where the dick pics come in.

I'm out of a long relationship, miscarried, and alone and someone sparks my attention, but that's another story. I was grieving and yet still able to be aroused and interested. Was it the hurt talking, did I just need to feel desired or loved? Nah, I am human and my interest was piqued. It was just a time when I was dealing with grief. While the imaginary love affair didn't last long, I was awakened and now wanted to be more of the old Myesha. I wanted to be strongly desired and devoured like I imagined. Shoot, I am still grieving, but I ain't dead is what I kept telling myself.

    When I started therapy over 4 years ago, I had no idea the transition I was going to make. I knew there was more, I knew that I was here for a higher purpose, and I knew life couldn't be so shitty. I had one therapist yawn during a few of my sessions; and shit, I understood why the yawn came because I was honestly tired of talking about the shit. However, you see why it takes someone so long to get help, some people really don't care. I would go home and listen to the tape of my assault twice a day and get up and go to work. Day in day out, I was still not really processing the grief of losing myself. Eventually, I got to the point where I could process without the emotions I tied to myself and see the event on a raw level which helped me process more than anything. I am not one for the fluff. Tell me the best way to process; even if it hurts I want to do the work. Currently, I am living with my needs and wants first and foremost. As a matter of fact, at this point, I am only concerned with what makes me happy. I followed the guidelines, I played the position I was given, I abided by the rules, and now it's time I do it my way. We use the motto that we only live once, but we live like we will be here forever. When I am asked where I see myself in 5 years, I now see a legacy, a way to make an impact and work in my purpose. I now ask others, what is their legacy? What will be known about us when we leave the physical? Immediately, I know if we are in alignment and move forward in purpose. I am building a network of like-minded creators, doers, changers, and healers. We are powerful, and it's refreshing to feel this way about life again. It is refreshing to know that I was able to shake the negative perceptions and limited views of myself.

    It was not with a weak heart that I started on the reflection of myself and how I dealt with grief. I always knew there was more to life, I knew that experiences only shape who we are, and that they did not dictate who we became. However, this is not what I was being told, this was not what was acceptable. You become what you have experienced. You are now this thing, so you should relate, react, and be this certain way. Wow, I can't tell you the inner turmoil this created. Seeing myself as something else that no one else could see. I was always called crazy, but by this point, I felt I really was. Being emotional did not make the processing of losing who I thought I was easy at all. Going back and forth with what the "masses" said, and what I knew and what I saw daily in the work I did with people. Someone was a liar, and it wasn't me. Once I got to that point, nothing anyone said to me was received unless it resonated. I didn't allow people to push their perceptions of me onto me. I took accountability for who I was, who I became, and who I decided I was going to be from now on.

    Take off! Let me tell you how it feels to be empowered and no longer living in the shadow of the thoughts of others. It's scary, it's exciting, it's emotional, it's powerful, it's contagious, it's hectic, it's calm, it's MFin' awesome! I see different, I think different, I process different, and I am apologetic for none of it. I do push myself in the efforts of healing and helping others. I do push myself to see more than what is put in front of me. I do push myself to be to others what I wish to have. I do push myself to be the best version of myself so that I can enjoy fully my time here on earth. I have to push myself in all these ways in order to stay in my power, in order to continue to bring change, in order to be accountable to myself in all the great things I am doing and will do and continue to be. I do push myself because the alternate I could not endure again knowing who I AM now! If everyone could see the actual damage and control that is inflicted on one other just with our thoughts and perceptions we would take back the power.

Grief doesn't always have to hurt! [I'll tell you about that shortly] However, now I grieve in appreciation. I have learned that I am so many things and that is ok. I appreciate all parts of me as I was created special and of God, so what else could be expected...

Remember the dick pic conversation? Well in grieving Myesha, I was also simultaneously grieving a long-term relationship and a miscarriage at the same time. In my grieving, I found excitement and happiness in who I remembered I ws----an openly sexual person that had a hell of an imagination! I was happy I got a glimpse of her. In grieving, we focus on the sorrow when we should also take time to see the bursts of the old you as it surfaces, and it will. TRUST ME!

This takes me to the point that grief doesn't have to hurt. Sometimes when I wanted to hurt instead I processed, I meditated, I reflected on everything great and in alignment with what I had been praying for. I have real live conversations with myself about ensuring I focus on the forward movement and mindset change that must occur. I know it may sound weird, but talking to yourself really does help! Once I sit in my emotions and analyze the situation, I am able to pick through the parts that need to be processed so that I can grow from that experience. I started to write about all the great things that were happening in spite of. I had to start finding the good and the things I could find joy in versus the negativity I did before. I had to change my mindset for this to occur, and I had to live in the experience of grief doesn't have to hurt, it can also carry so much joy and little burst of happiness.

In less than a year, I have accomplished so much despite the grief I had to grind through. Imagine how powerful I could be without the grief, I'm just saying. From this perspective I know nothing other than the fact that I am a creator and no one can tell me otherwise! Our limitations are only our own, no one can stop us once we are in alignment, in faith, in purpose, and with the Universe, the Higher Power, or GOD. I'm not religious, but I have a testimony and growth to prove it. I have accomplished so much in the last 90 days because I chose to do the work! Someone can give you 10 easy steps to make $100, but you still have to make it happen. I wanted to quit, shut down, deny anything better than what I already had at one point in time and now, I am just different. I value different, I follow different, I lead different, I listen different, I hear different. I know what I am up against, but I also know the power in ME and of those I influence. I am not trying to change anyone's mind about limitations, fear, grief, accountability, dreams, mental illness, unity, religion, spirituality, career, or dreams, I'm just living my experience hoping to influence who I can by being who I am authentically.

In my growth in the last year (actually 90 days), I was able to see past my past, yes past my past, and move forward in my greatness. I have been blessed and aligned to join so many courageous, powerful, and enlightened networks of people and organizations. Having a network of talented and aligned spirits has been a blessing and trumps any monetary desire. My goal is impact, influence, growth and empowerment. Exposure is all I have so I must only work with those in alignment with my vision. Embarking on my purpose beyond grief has empowered me to complete so many things I never did before... I am sharing so you know you can do it too, you can create and be whatever you wish, don't believe me...just watch! Grief doesn't own you, nor does it owe you anything!

Remember how I said you could be lost and not even know it. Well I was Gold and did not even know it at some point.

I was living my life trying to fit into the mold and be all regular and shit. Always being told I was different, weird, emotional, bossy, controlling, and crazy shaped who I was. All those things are a part of me and all those things make me the best Myesha. There is no other Myesha, there is no one like me, I am unique, I am valuable, I am capable, I am healing, and I am needed, so I'm telling the world! In grinding through my grief, I have impacted others. I have seen the women in the Blue Girl Turned Gold Vol 1 start to embark on their highest good and share the mission of women empowerment. It is so dope! The women in from Grief to Grind, the elite 8, the powerful things they are already doing and the abundance for them that is yet to come. The Entrepreneurs in Reclaiming my Time from the 9 to 5 Grind and how they will influence and lead others. The cuffs of shame and the power that will be released with Releasing the Shackles of Shame…do you see the power in healing yet? Do you see the power in choosing you? Do you see where you can take a step in the way of creating your own .

    Processing in appreciation of who I am becoming has been my focus. I have bad days, good days, great days and shitty days, but at the end of the day I have the end of the day! I am creating the life I desire. While it is uncomfortable I love seeing myself grow. Four years ago, I didn't see this Myesha, 1 year ago I still didn't clearly see her, but she is showing up and showing out now. I am appreciative of my transparency, I am appreciative in my willingness to accept myself- my WHOLE self, I am appreciative of my support of and in myself, I am appreciative of my creative spirit, I am appreciative of my giving heart, I am appreciative in my humanity nature, I am appreciate of Wynter Snow (google her), I and just living my best life in appreciation, GRIEF has had enough of my mf time!

    Grinding for self is so satisfying, it's so empowering, it's so exciting, is so mf hard…well the start up anyway. On January 1, 2018 I started giving 100% percent energy and focus to my nonprofit, my personal brand, and Myesha 2018 refurbished but certified model! With my account in the negative I obtained a Passion Pushing Coach Ms. Andrea A. Moore, I signed up for her 90 days to greatness program and within 15 days I had done the work of the 90 day program as far as obtaining goals. Grinding and grieving, but grieving in appreciation. The alignment Andrea has with me and my purpose is surreal. I met her in a Facebook group and she signed on to the Blue Girl Turned Gold Anthology. Now, she was my coach and helping me push my passion. She helped me further the adjustments needed to my mindset. She gave me the ok to take the fuck off basically!

I have been experiencing so many great things since learning how to process my grief. I have been able to take back my future and draw the lane that I am in. Ten years ago, I couldn't see where I sit today, but where I see myself in ten years has a much clearer view. At any time I could have changed my mindset, at any time I could have gotten up and created the exact day I wanted. This newfound power in letting go and grieving properly has shown me that the Myesha I was didn't have shit on the Myesha I am now and I rejoice in that! Seeing yourself different is the only way to be the self you wish to see. I am living my best life with no apologies or explanations. I have decided to only work towards things that are positive gains for which I am shaping myself to be. It's a mindset thing and the sooner you get it the better. I am just getting it at 38, but the blessing is for me to teach others this so they aren't stuck in themselves as long as I was. So we have Myesha the new and improved model here and despite the experiences I had, despite what ails I allowed in my life, despite what decisions I made, despite all the areas where I sold MYESHA short, we made it! We still have a way to go, but working from this view is more optimistic. I don't have grief blocking my grind and shit!
So I had to let her go, the Myesha that had the fear of speaking, she had to be released. The Myesha that believed in the shame she was taught had to be released.

The Myesha that believed the false illusion that she was NOT stronger than her struggles had to be released. Releasing that burden of trying to be the Myesha everyone else wanted was a great relief. To know that all this time I could have chosen this at any moment empowers me to help others. The same choice can be made by anyone, but we don't see it. How do I know this? I didn't see it, BUT now I do. I chose to be a better me for me. I am humbled, honored and appreciative that you took the time to see my grind and my grief. I hope this empowers you to choose you and see differently.

CHAPTER SEVEN

Is There A Rainbow At The End Of The Storm

How did I get here? I just kept repeating it in my head. How did I get here? I was nice. I helped people in this community. I volunteered, and I worked so hard to make a difference. Here I am lying flat on my back in an emergency room after my first ambulance ride, praying to God Almighty that I hadn't had a full-blown heart attack. Yet there go all my clothes in every direction, everyone talking at once, and everyone running and working with great urgency. Their haste made me more nervous than what was happening. Maybe I was dying, and I was too silly to realize it. The past 24 hours rolled through my mind in slow motion.

The day before my daughter Elizabeth asked me to watch some program with her that she had on DVR. It was about lunchtime, and she offered to make a frozen pizza with spicy sausage on it. I bought it a few days before. She and her brother had just returned home for the summer from college. I enjoyed the fact that she wanted to spend time with me; but, since I was having such a great amount of stress in my life at the time, I enjoyed the time with her. We hashed over some of the stressful events that had been occurring. I knew I felt frustrated just talking about it because my turmoil rolled onto her, and it wasn't her fault. I knew these times would come to an end and she would no longer live at home. I was so blessed as she was everything I was times ten. She was and still is funny, sweet, always kind to others, yet fiercely loyal, and such a good friend. We enjoyed the show and the time together. A few hours later I said, "I think that pizza gave me heartburn." This was a very unusual occurrence for me as I had only had it 2 times in 3 total pregnancies. It continued throughout the night.

Nothing I tried to treat it -worked at all. In fact, at some time around midnight or 1:00am, I opened my phone up because I was so uncomfortable and started searching sites like WEBMD.

All the comments were referring to a possible heart problem. Weird? My heart didn't hurt, or my arm, or my neck as you would typically think. Just a burning feeling like heartburn was all I felt. I decided there was only one medicine I hadn't tried, and I set my alarm for 7am (when the local grocery opened) to go purchase it. I promised myself if I didn't feel way better by 8am when the doctor's office opened, I would call. Unfortunately for me, 8:00AM rolled around with me making an appointment for 8:30, which I drove myself to. I went in and had my blood pressure taken, and it was much higher than it had ever been. I started to feel very nervous. She said, "I think we will do an EKG", and wheeled a machine in.

Very quick test and she smiled and said, "Congratulations, you've won a free ride to the emergency room!", as if that were a great thing. She told me my readings were abnormal and she wanted to be safe. I said, "Why can't I drive there? I drove here." That didn't happen. She called my husband for me, and he agreed to meet the ambulance there. I had never been in an ambulance, but now I can tell you it's bumpy, loud, and feels very surreal. The EMT took my blood pressure again, and it was sky high. I said, "Are you kidding me?" "Nope!", he said and put a nitro tab under my tongue. I was two days from turning 50 years old, and I just couldn't understand how this was happening.

    This couldn't be my life! A few minutes later, the EMT asked what my pain level was now. I said meekly, "Zero". I was just fully realizing my heart in my own body was betraying me. During the rest of the 25-minute ambulance ride, I prayed, tried to simply clear my mind, and focus on what was happening in my body. Upon arrival at the hospital, I had never seen such a frenzy of activity. On one hand, I was relieved to see them so concerned; but, because I literally felt no pain, I was unclear as to why everyone seemed to feel like I was at death's door. And there go my clothes with 2-3 people talking to me at one time. I had an emergency heart catheter to look at my heart while about five people waited and watched to see what the next move would be. The heart doctor who was on call in the ER said, "Have you had any major stress, a death of a loved one, or death of a spouse recently?

I laughed out loud and said, "Does character assassination count?" He laughed and said, "Maybe, if that is stressful to you."

Well, stressful wasn't even close to covering it. He went on to explain that I had what was called "Broken Heart Syndrome". This is typically seen in much older couples who have been married forever and suddenly one is lost and the other one dies of a "broken heart". This is ultimately what killed Debbie Reynolds after Carrie Fisher's death. It literally causes a compression in the heart. Mine was in the left ventricle which he showed me on the monitor. The great news was that I had not had a heart attack. The bad news was I was being admitted for a few days for monitoring, and I had to reduce my stress. "Okay, so if I am leaving to drive for vacation in Florida for 7 days, and then coming back and in the next 7 days moving out of the house I have lived in for over 20 years, this will probably NOT qualify for stress free living, right?", I asked. He responded to me with, "Well I can't tell you not to move, but I can tell you to just point and tell people what to do!" Well this was quite the turn of events. Probably the most interesting thing about all of this is that the move was being done to leave all the stress behind. I thought I was being proactive in managing the stress. I thought I had put it all behind me. My mind wandered back to the previous 4 years and where this all truly started.

Back in November of 2011, the small town I lived in, which I will refer to as Tiny Town, was in a bit of an uproar. As sometimes occurs in smaller towns, some voices were louder than others, and political problems were occurring. I was a member of the local Chamber of Commerce at the time because I was a home-based business owner- I joined to grow my business and make connections. I was just starting to get more involved in the chamber and actively participating. I had recently met the mayor during a meeting. He genuinely seemed like a nice person and was very active in the community. The Chamber secretary and one of the other board members suggested I run for city council in my ward. I laughed and said I will see if Scott will. Scott is my husband, and I felt he was better suited for that position. I heard through friends that there needed to be a change, and I felt from what I was hearing that perhaps my representation was not to my liking.

I was encouraged to run for the position myself. I had many people who came up to me and told me to do it. Since I hadn't even talked to them, this might have been my first clue that Tiny Town had quite a communication network that I was unaware of. That December, I turned in my paper with the required signatures to run for my council seat because I had set a New Year's Resolution that year to not complain about anything unless I was willing to do something about it. As I rolled into 2012, I campaigned and won the seat easily. I learned the new role and truly enjoyed my four years in that position. There were a few bumps in the road with people being derogatory, but I let it roll off. I knew who I was and whose I was. I remained rooted in my faith, which was about to be extremely needed. For many months in late 2014, the political climate in Tiny Town became increasingly volatile and nasty. While I loved serving, I was really resisting running again. I had multiple people on the council asking me to please run again, and if I wanted to vacate at some point, they would appoint someone to the seat after I won. My head told me not to do it. I warred with myself, and I caved to what they wanted not what I wanted, and that was where I got myself onto the wrong road. I learned at that point in time to listen to that inner nudging, as it is from God. I did what was best for them not what was best for me. Interestingly, God had other plans for me, because I believe he knew I wouldn't leave, so he created obstacles which caused me to have to leave to save myself. The campaign trail became ridiculous. I had 50 political signs when I started, and I ended up with like 18 or 20. People stole them, picked them up out of the ground, and laid them down at night. Then, the social media slaughter started. I was okay with what anyone said until they started maligning my children.

I was running for a public office not asking people to attack my children. I was truly struggling to maintain my composure. I was internalizing it because I wasn't going to spew negativity back. That is not in my nature. I was secure that I had served and served well, honorably, and with integrity. I volunteered so many hours with my church and my community that the hours surely counted into the thousands. I chaired a community festival for four years, two of which, I received no compensation for the hundreds of hours I worked. A harsh cut came when all those thousands of hours of volunteer service to the community were diminished by one letter to the editor published in the Tiny Town newspaper. The letter suggested I had only volunteered to make myself look good. Emotionally, I was battered, bruised, and hurt. Social media posts were taking its toll on me. People sent me screenshots of Facebook posts which really did not help me emotionally. It all felt like thousands of pounds. I guess because I was keeping most of it to myself, my heart said no, we don't like this.

    The final blow came shortly before the election. I am a Christian and attended church regularly at the same place for nearly 13 years in Tiny Town. The pastor asked for prayers, and we were to put them in the offering plate. I put in to please help me get through the election. I want to be extremely clear. I never cared if I won. I didn't really want to be part of it anymore. This probably didn't help me in the race. I didn't walk my ward because my record should have served me. Unfortunately, church was part of the battleground. I had people who wouldn't talk to me anymore, wouldn't look at me, etc. It was no longer a safe place. It no longer held any sanctuary for me. This was very hard considering how many hours I had put in on committees, funeral dinners, chaperoning mission trips, etc. After asking for that prayer request, I never heard from anyone in my church. To add insult to injury, when I was hospitalized and spent 3 days there- and right through my 50th birthday, not a single person came to see me or called from my church. I received zero support through the bashing of my character or through the loss of the election which didn't matter so much. It was painful to realize I didn't matter at all in my own church. I did ask God what I had done to find myself in this position. Everything seemed very unclear to me.

    In the span of 4 weeks, all my service to the community had been thrown in the garbage, and I no longer felt welcome in my own church. My children, my marriage, and every other part of my life were attacked through social media. I lost an election and almost had a heart attack. The final piece was I had separated myself emotionally from pretty much everything and everyone. I did have God's armor though. I knew I did not deserve what I had received. In that same span of time, I quit every single position including being on the chamber board, managing their social media, and all other community volunteer positions, including church. I retreated inside myself.

Ironically, I told my husband 2 weeks before the election that I couldn't live there. I asked if he was coming with me. One might see that as an ultimatum, but I saw it as I needed to find alignment again. I did not fit in Tiny Town. I don't think I ever fit in Tiny Town, but I wasn't aware of it. He reminded me that he loved me, and he would go wherever I wanted. This was a big statement as we had a very large yard that he had cultivated into beautiful gardens. We had invested 20 years of our lives renovating and restoring our big, beautiful old house. At Christmas time, we were even on the tour of homes which raised money for the community and had a couple thousand people through our home. We put up seven Christmas trees every year and decorated every room. Was it all for nothing?

Well, that is what I thought of course. The old saying "you can't see the forest for the trees" was my life at that moment. I completely understand the journey now. The one piece of the puzzle that I haven't shared was that my job was one of the things that helped save me. Two years prior to this mess, I joined a new company in the network marketing industry. I was not looking for anything new, but it was looking for me. I rejected it the first time I saw it. God had other plans for me because He knew what was coming, even though I didn't. He planted this product called The Thrive experience in my life because He knew I would not only need the product for my body, but He knew I was going to desperately need to have the people who would ultimately support me through the difficult storm that was coming. Joining Le-Vel and sharing the Thrive experience became so important to me in the year and a half before the storm. I met and connected with thousands of happy, healthy, positive-minded, and strong people. Not only were these people in my upline support systems, but on my own team. This piece is literally what kept me going through the storm, aside from my immediate family. Because it was such a fabulous and positive environment, it helped me see what a detrimental place Tiny

Town was for me personally. It was kind of like light and dark. I gravitated to the light and began to shift, grow, and emerge like a caterpillar emerges from a cocoon. I continued to work, but we immediately started looking for a place to move. We went in full on move mode as a family. I suppose looking back, this may have contributed to the hospital event. It was still stress, just a different kind. We had to move 20 years' worth of stuff, and that's stressful within itself.

While lying on that exam table and hearing the doctor tell me I was lucky, and I was going to have to reduce my stress, I thought, I AM reducing my stress. I pondered whether I was running away from my troubles, but in my heart, I felt certain that I was running to something. I felt like I was saving myself. This feeling was completely accurate.

    As I posted pictures on social media of our moving trucks with stuff packed in it, some people in the community were shocked. Many sent private messages. While that was nice, it was too late to have any impact. Many people apologized for other people's behavior, which was sort of ironic. It was time for healing. I mean in a physical and emotional way as well. I never set foot back in that church until our son decided to get married there two years later. In fact, it took over 6 months for me to walk into a church at all. I listened to lots of sermons online, etc., so it wasn't as if I was without His word, but I just couldn't bring myself to go inside. For a short time, we attended the church we went to prior to moving to Tiny Town, but my husband and I both felt uneasy. We were both hearing subtle grumblings about trouble with egotistical behaviors on staff, and I nicely said I was out. We decided to attend Hope Church, and that was ultimately one of things that led to becoming whole again. I give great thanks to Beth Yokely, who was and still is the Connections pastor, for inviting me to breakfast. This was a whole year and a half after everything happened. As I shared my story with her, she understood as I cried in the IHOP. (That wasn't embarrassing at all.) I was slightly perplexed as I shared that it still emotionally hurt so much and still felt a bit raw after 18 months.

    She said, "Well you shouldn't be surprised you are grieving. There isn't any time limit on that". This was truly when the lightbulb went off for me. I don't think she honestly knew how important that moment was for me. I had never once considered that what I had been through was grief. Maybe it was simply tough to see it through the anger and disappointment. I felt like I dropped a hundred pounds off my shoulders that day that I didn't even know was there. Scott and I went for a very long walk that evening in our neighborhood. I shared what Beth and I had talked about. I looked at him, and I said, "I had no idea! Grief? Seriously, today I realized why this has been so hard. I died! Literally, who I thought I was and who I believed myself to be, is dead and gone. I am not 100% sure who I am anymore."

It was where my healing began. I started sorting through what I knew about myself. I was a natural leader. I loved people and I loved helping. This was one of the reasons my Le-Vel business was so important to me and continued to help me both physically and emotionally. My strongest qualities were still being utilized in my business, but I missed volunteering and being part of that kind of community. The only volunteering, I didn't quit was working with the Forever Home Feline Ranch. This is a feline rescue. I've learned that animals never emotionally hurt you, and rarely do the people who volunteer through them either. I still help them today because I love cats. I needed to be able to spend time where I was accepted for me in whatever damaged way I showed up. This was the case with the Feline Ranch, Hope Church, and in my business. I began taking some baby steps in new opportunities. I helped with a couple small things at Hope Church. My circle of friends had become much smaller. I didn't count, but I estimate at least 50- 75 people had unfriended me on Facebook from Tiny Town, which was fine. A good friend told me it was the trash taking itself out. I don't know about that, but I focus on who brings me good energy in my life now. I surround myself only with people who pour into me in a positive way and who support me emotionally.

As I reflect on all the personal attacks and incredibly hard events that led up to today, I realize that God had a plan for me all along. The problem was that I was not going to be able to do what I was called to do from where I was. He created the storms to push me to make a change I wasn't going to make for a few years, but His timing was to push me to do it just then. I realized that I wasn't strong enough to withstand some of the trials I would face, until I went through the fire. Through that fire, I have become a writer, an author, a blogger, a better speaker, trainer, and motivator. I am more sympathetic and kind to others. I am physically healthier as well. My power of discernment is so much better. I never tried to hurt people intentionally, so I incorrectly assumed other people wouldn't either. Hurting people hurt others- which is why I knew I had to heal fully to be able to help others. Beth helped me to see that I had to honestly acknowledge my grief for what it was and find a place to embrace it and learn from it. This served me very well in my business, as it has continued to flourish as I have become more aware of not hiding my own pain. Since this very painful incident, I have reached the top rank of my company and enjoyed so many new opportunities that I could not have imagined being a part of. When I first saw Andrea A. Moore post about this compilation of stories, I immediately thought, this is my story, even though it's not traditional grief. Ironically after we initially talked, I decided not to do it. God promptly put a reminder right in front of me showing me that people were still talking negatively about me. He showed me I prospered because it was His plan not theirs. I immediately sent her a message and said I would do it.

When I flash back to that time in the ambulance where I pondered, how did I get here, I realize it was never about the how. It was all about the why and the purpose for my life. I live every day to the fullest now and work to crush every goal I set. I solidly stand in my purpose to help others, no matter what others try to do to me or say about me. It was the storms He sent that ultimately created the rainbows in my life today. I know now it was all part of the process of His plan for my personal grief to grind journey.

If my story helps even one person persevere through the turmoil, tough times, and grief, it will be worth it. I wrote this scared and a bit unsure, but I have come to understand I no longer care about what someone else thinks of me or what they say about me. My truth and my walk are mine! Another growth point for me, and I'm happy about it.

CHAPTER EIGHT

Redeemed

It started at a young age, insecurity I mean, when it seemed like everyone around me had "it" all together; meanwhile I was still a garden flower child awaiting the day to be "picked" so I too can see my worth and purpose in this world; but that never happened. Surrounded by people with conceited mindsets, popular reputations, and petite body shapes, made my little insecurities become ugly flaws. It didn't help hearing that I needed to use Vaseline because I have stretch marks either. I pretty much went through my adolescent years being insecure and embarrassed about what I looked like in others eyes. With most baggage comes more problems and that is where insecurity introduced me to shame.

Things I did as a young lady that was completely innocent was taunted by my peers. "You a little too big to be wearing those shorts." Or my favorite "You need to wear stuff that suits your body more." At that age I did not realize that I was being body shamed by women ten sizes smaller or ten sizes bigger than me. I remember staring at my body in the mirror one time with curiosity and confusion. "why does my waist curve in this way? Why is my butt darn near on my back? Why does everyone think negatively about me just because I have curves at the age of 10?" Things I was **TAUGHT** to be ashamed about because the people around me, family, friends, classmates, and peers, spoke things that influenced me to.

That entire year I tried my best to avoid mirrors while getting dressed for school. I would stand in front of my closed door with my back turned against the mirrors and I would get dressed with the lights off, to avoid catching a glance of my "stretch marks." My shame eventually turned into guilt and regret by the time I was in the eighth grade; this was the beginning of the chaos insecurity brought along in the baggage deal. I was mistaken for a grown woman a lot when I was in the eighth grade, from my looks to personality, but being a fourteen year old in the eighth grade was the only thing I was focused on before all of my friends and I go our separate ways for high school. "Hooting and hollering," was a common thing I heard when I was outside with my friends or even the now casual stares from men when I would walk to the corner store; I was unfazed by it because my mentality was never focused that way. However, there were many people that were fazed by the unwanted attention I received; and this began to be one of the worst times of my life. Hearing these ratchet loud mouthed raspy voiced heifers constantly yell threats at me throughout the hallways and consistently harassed me after school, was the start of a terrible, depressed me. Everyday these girls would just find something to pick on me about. "Yo' dirty ass", "her nappy-ass hair", "Girl did you see her shoes? They had scuff marks all over them!" was the common remarks I heard from these ashy elbow awkwardly shaped heifers.

    I would never respond, though I should have, and they used my silence as their strength to keep bothering me and eventually it became way too much; the first suicidal thought I had ever had. It was just a thought, nothing too deep but just a simple, "what if?" On top of all the bullying going on at school, I would try my hardest to go home and avoid the threats, bullying, and degrading remarks I received when she had one too many drinks; every day. "You betta' not be scared of those bitches, shit as big as you are, I'm surprised they even wanna' start with you." she said between slurred words. Thanks! Exactly what I needed to be body shamed again. Was it not bad enough that I have yet to actually look at myself in the mirror but now I am being treated the same way at home that I am at school? This was a daily routine, be degraded and targeted at home because of too much Korbel and be threatened and harassed at school because of too much jealousy. Why couldn't they understand that the way I dress was not based on my style but on what my family could afford? Why couldn't she understand that I can't stand up to the bullies at school because I have yet to stand up to my first bully at home? I felt let down a lot by what my friends could do with their mothers that I never did. I wish I could have those girl talks and empowerment conversations about how I can be and do anything I want when I get older; but no I was **told** I was going to be a lawyer and that was the end of that conversation. I did not have a say so in many of the choices growing up, not even my own individuality. I was reminded many times throughout my adolescent years that "I didn't have anything without it being given to me, that I was dependent, that I didn't have a pot to piss in or a window to throw it out of, that everything, even the clothes bought for me and the room I slept in, was NOT mine. I have nothing to offer." In all my identity, who I was, what I sought after in life did not matter unless I was given the say so. Damn, I wasn't even allowed to like what I like without it being criticized or completely disregarded as unimportant. (so I've been told.)

      To grow up with little to no identity is dangerous, because I like many filled myself up with the trends and ways of the world. I didn't have a true identity, but maybe I could finesse one like I have always been shown by the ones claiming to be "more important" than me. By high school, I had met a lot of new friends and a lot of new outlets to avoid what I had been internalizing. I began partying and drinking at the age of fifteen with a few of the girls that I grew up with from the same neighborhood. It all was a great escape from the nonsense and bullshit I would have to deal with at home and school. For the first time in my life I felt like I was in control of what I could do and no one had the say so to tell me different. When anger meets alcohol, the person birthed under the influence is the person longing to be heard and understood. My drunkenness was a great time though. I laughed hard, I partied hard, but most importantly, I wasn't me. I was no longer that girl that everyone bullied, I was no longer that girl that was being degraded by drunken slurs, I was a different person, the only person even I envied. I was confident, likeable, unbothered, and honest. I voiced my opinion and didn't take shit from anybody. If anyone had a problem with the drunken me, they would be cut by my words or bruised by these hands; either way I was ready for whatever. Although I hated to hurt people's feelings, my feelings were hurt and this is where misery met company. I had a few people that I considered like family and that I entrusted more with my secrets than my own family, so we were always together hanging out, laughing, clubbing, etc. With most kick-backs, mutual friends or family members perhaps, would come and hang out with us all at either a friend's house or elsewhere. I trusted my group of friends enough to know that I would be protected in case of something happening to me, however, something about this particular night changed. A family member of one of my friends was hanging out at our mutual friend's house as well, and because I knew him from childhood, I was unfazed by his being there. At least I thought I could be.

Somehow the drink I received from said "friend" was laced with a drug that had me passed out on my friends' enclosed porch. With my conscientiousness fading out and in, leaving me feeling completely lifeless, I tried my hardest to wake up and go home; I mean I **literally** lived around the corner. However, whatever was in my drink made my entire body slumped and too heavy to move; I passed back out for a moment and was awakened by a familiar voice. "You alright Neesh?" Because that was a nickname only few people gave me. I do not remember responding but the voice was now speaking and sitting right across from me. "You good Neshia?" The voice asked again, and it was then that I knew who was speaking to me. "I'm hot, I need to go home, I need to throw up, and I don't feel good." I **remember** saying these words to them. "Nah, just take your jacket off, that's why you so hot." The voice said. I was still slumped over on the couch, I tried waking myself up but my body felt lifeless, like I have been numbed and paralyzed. What had seemed like a few minutes that passed by, he was now sitting in front of me. "You said you wanna go home Neesh?" he asked as if he didn't hear me the first time. "Yeah, I wanna go home, I'm about to go home." I muttered in between trying to catch my breath and not throw up all over my friend's porch. I then asked him if he could tell my best friend, at the time that I wanted to leave. It seemed as if whatever this was that was making me feel this way was not letting up anytime soon, and all I wanted was to be home, in my bed, without a care in the world. Passing out made everything around me silent, but it was in this moment when my conscientiousness woke up abruptly to what was taking place. "Stop! What are you doing?" I was beyond shocked. "C'mon Neesh, you knew I been liking you since we was kids." **His exact words**. Those words I can still hear. Those words I can curse him for even speaking. Those words that reminded me it was **my fault** for him liking me and me not returning that same interest.

Those words that made him feel justified for sexually assaulting me on our friend's porch. What do I do in this moment? I am drunk and being raped with no strength to fight him off of me. "Get off of me!" I screamed as loud as I could. "Man, what's yo problem man, you knew I been liking you and instead you like my cousin!" his exact words. "Get off of me please! I just want to go home!" I said fighting back tears and pushing him off of me. "Mann a'ight." He sounded disappointed. For some reason that event made me wake up enough to get myself out of there. I pulled my underclothes and pants, which were around my ankles, back up and sped walked home. I didn't know how to feel. I was so in shock by what just happened, it had not even sunk in that I was just raped. Was "your liking for me" justifiable to rape me? I used to get drunk many times, I never thought about raping someone. I had been to the wildest of parties, I never once thought about raping someone. I have had the biggest crush on someone before, I never thought about raping them. Why is this only justifiable for you; because you "liked me since we were kids?" I just turned 16. What is not fair; you having the nerve to smile knowing you stole someone else's. The fact that you can even look at yourself and not see anything wrong with what you did justified my reasoning for not trusting anyone, ever again. You have got to be out of your mind to believe what you did was okay. You broke me in ways you cannot understand. I felt so ashamed for what happened. Every feeling of regret, guilt, shame, humiliation, anger, rage, and disgust filled me and the very little confidence I had with being under the influence was completely ripped away.

You encountered my body in ways you had no right to and the worst part is that you felt obligated based off of what you felt was fair?! You disgust me! You don't have a right to MY

BODY! There is NEVER an excuse! You preyed on me and you stole from me. You stole my dignity, and my vulnerability. I get angry thinking about it. I find myself crying over something I believed for a long while was my fault. I'm in here crying out to God because I don't know how to feel. I thought it was my fault because I had a half cup of strong liquor, until wisdom said, "It doesn't justify what has happened." Here I am making fucking excuses for the bullshit you decided to do to me, and you have the nerve to say the reason you did it is because you "liked me but I liked your cousin!?" What in the hell?! Do you not know how illiterate you sound? How desperate and disgusting you present yourself?! If it had not been Jesus on my side because I promise; you ain't worth my life! I could call you everything but a child of God; you did everything the devil would desire. You stole from me; you killed my security, and destroyed my peace of mind. I struggled for years to pick myself up and begin to unfold the reasoning for my hidden anger and why I despised people being too close to me. I had to educate myself on the post effects for rape and sexual assault alone and with my counselor. They say 'it is never your fault regardless of what you had to drink or what you were wearing, a rapist is a rapist.' There is no excuse for you or what you have done. No excuse.

And as unfortunate to admit, you were not the first person to steal my innocence; and innocence is not always referred to physical contact. My innocence was taken from me. All the insecurities, all the pain, all the misguidance, all veered from my stolen innocence. I relied on my close peers to teach me things about myself even just being a young woman and I feel completely let down. I should be able to ask questions about the things I feel and are experiencing without being bashed and shunned for it. "Are you doing something? Then you don't need to worry about it then!" should not be the answer a young woman seeking advice from her mother should be.

Every piece of me has been used in abusive ways. I never had the opportunity to embrace being the woman I am because the younger girl in me is still broken and ashamed for the things that happened to her that she never got to explain or receive closure from. I hate this. I loathe this feeling as if I am wrong or immature because I still seek answers about things "a woman should already know." But I can't because I have been taught to be ashamed for being open and honest about how I feel and what I feel. I feel so let down by the people I expected to play the role they so arrogantly profess. I watched my friends experience their childhood with nothing less than joy, but mine was limited because although adolescent, my body reflected as "grown woman." Friends expected for me to be the "conceited girl" because I had the look and figure they only dreamt about, but the truth is, I envied them growing up. Boys would get them flowers and nice things just for them being their girlfriends. Meanwhile I couldn't trust anyone that wanted to date me because I was under the impression from family and friends that "the only reason they wanna be with you is because you have a nice body." This is why worthlessness had always had a way into my mentality. I was considered only valuable enough to be someone's girlfriend because of my body shape. And to see how people reacted towards me was one thing but for my own mother to look at me with despise in her eyes, based off of what other people thought of me. I was her embarrassment.

I realize that a lot of times I would argue with my mother, it would never stay on topic of the argument; it would instantly turn into intimidation and degrading matters. Nose to Nose in my face cursing me and reminding me of how I could never amount to who she is, stepping on my foot while cursing me to remind me that "I can't do shit about it,", and words that bruised me deeper than any drunken slap across the face could ever leave. I accepted that I could only amount to something under her approval, and everything and anything I ever could imagine being would only be appropriate if it was because of her that I made it to where I am.

There is a young girl inside of me that is fed up and grieving. Grieving because everything she was ever taught growing up turned out to be a lie and fed up because she is sick and tired of relying, trusting, forgiving the very people that continues to dig the grave for who she is and the gifts she possesses. It's as if these very people refuses for me to believe that I have a purpose and calling on my life. It's as if these very people do not ever want me to live because once I do begin to live, their lies and manipulation will become exposed. It's as if these people only wanted me to see through the eyes of their opinion of me because they are angry with where they are in life. I get afraid sometimes; what if I become great and these people never speak to me again? Lord, these people are my family, the ones you ordained in my life.

Father, why would you send people that you knew was going to hurt me and make me believe that I was less than what you call me?!? But then you taught me something about purpose. You said in your word "... in all things God works for the good of those who love him, who have been called according to his purpose." (Romans 8:28). Now Lord, I have always loved you and yet I didn't know you. I have always claimed you, yet I did not speak about you. Why in this moment of despair and surrender, you rescue me from the very trap set out to kill me? I am a wretched undone and a working progress altogether, surely you cannot expect for someone like me to be called according to your purpose? I couldn't understand it. I have been searching in people for the exact things only someone greater could have given me. However, I was consistently moving in circles, because my reality was in disagreement with my mentality. Reality was proving to me that I was far from where I have bee, but my mentality refused to believe the good was true and it continuously reverted me back to my past.

Everyone just thought I had "an attitude problem." "Neshia why you always gotta' make a big deal when somebody say or do something bogus to you damn it ain't that serious." Words said to me by my own brother. But brother if only you knew how angry I was with you for not protecting me from something you had no control over. Anger meets Blame. I blamed everyone for my mistakes, I blamed everyone for my pain, I blamed everyone for my insecurities. It was always someone else's fault for why I felt the way that I did. I gave up on being that shy innocent girl I once was. I did not care if my family resented my ways. I hated everything about me and I was falling apart. I am breaking and no one is helping me get up. Every friend I once had left my side. My family no longer wanted anything to do with me, they were all focused on their own interests and mine seemed obsolete and irrelevant to them. People I once looked at as family would not even return a phone call. I was so hurt I was so angry and I was completely and utterly alone with my brokenness. Betrayal from friendships, heart breaks from relationships, let downs by family members, side eyes from church members, and failures on school reports wiped what was left of me. I had no more fight left in me, this was it, I was going to end everything today.

Too much anxiety, too much hurt, too much this, too much that, too much of everything. I didn't know what I was going to do or how I was going to do it but the only thing that made sense to me in this state of mind was to take a shower.

While in there, something told me to, "just breathe." Eventually my quick and short breaths became long quivering inhales and for the first time in my life I felt the weight of my baggage on my shoulders; heavy, burdened, too much to bear. I cried, I screamed, I was on my knees on the floor of my bathtub. "I give up God, I can't do this anymore." I wept I fell on rock bottoms' floor and begged God to take my life for me. I was convinced that a disgrace like me could never inherit what God so willingly offered. I have lied, hurt, and dishonored God and so many others. I surrendered to God, I told him that this burden was too much to carry, this pain was too entangled to fix, this anger was too ferocious to heal, and there was no point in God wasting space for me being here. I was worthless.

    The only way I could think of ending this pain was death. But because I am what you call a "scary cat" I could not imagine seeing blood leave my wrists or hearing my heart beat slow down to nothing as my body fought to throw up an over-dosage of painkillers, so instead I asked the boldest question I have ever asked God, "Father, can you do me one last thing, after I fall asleep,…please don't wake me up tomorrow." I lay with my eyes closed and mentally re-encountered everything I had been through. Maybe I am as horrible of a person people make me out to be. Do they even care that I hurt and cry too? Was I supposed to feel like this? I mean I am used to being the strong one but now I am experiencing something that I have never experienced before. Maybe I do come off completely opposite than what I am intending to do. Why am I just now seeing this? Have I been this oblivious to reality that I am just now realizing that life does not come with a rewind button; or was that all just in my head? I have ruined some great opportunities, friendships, and moments. All of these instances replayed in my head and claimed the victory every time.

Surrender meet Christ. My mind had been filled with the remembrance of the adversities that I could not begin to understand until I got older. What made adversity hard was the fact that I had always been a sensitive person. My feelings are easily hurt and my raging anger would be the way I expressed it. However, as I became an adult, my sensitivity to words and the tones of others voices were at its most fragile; it had me walking out the door before they could finish their sentence. Even the slightest feeling of wrong energy made my anxiety level shift to a higher altitude. I was so uneased and frantic; I thought this was the point where people had mental breakdowns.

Yet, it was here in my broken, rock-bottom rigidness that I found God. No, it was not at church, I did not have a relationship with Christ other than hoping he would let me live because I had one too many drinks and I might not make it. But something about being in the position of surrender and despair, I felt his presence. I had never understood what they meant in church by 'being in the presence of God.' I just assumed that meant to bow your head and close your eyes when you pray; by the way that is actually humility. I did not hear about the part where God would show up in the midst of my troubles; the troubles I created. I was beyond convinced, because this was all of my mess, and my entire fault, God would never help me out of these situations. There was no way that God would forgive the unforgivable, there is no way that God could love the unlovable, there is absolutely no way that God could qualify the unqualified; so I thought. The lies I accepted about myself convinced me that God had already turned his face from me and that I was better off falling into the hands of the world and allowing it to do what-ever to me; because I lacked the knowledge of the armor it takes to be properly equipped for this fight I would soon enter into.

I received guidance from my mother-in-love about all the things that I was thinking and feeling and many times she had to talk some sense into me and calm my tears. I expressed to her my anger with God and my frustration with my upbringing. I had a difficult time trying to understand how they very exact people that judged me before are now and becoming the exact same things, and YET still look down on me? How could God see everything I was going through and yet I still had to fight alone? How could people use scriptures to condemn me but still want me to pray? How could God tolerate the nonsense everyone else did, but he has no patience or forgiveness for me? With all of these questions and hurt I was throwing at her, she smiled and told me one of the most profound things anyone has ever taught me "do not let anyone Define who God is to you!"

These words eventually began resonating in my heart and eventually took the place of the broken words that have been deeply rooted in me. This helped me begin my armor building because it made me instantly protect my way of understanding the truth about who God is and who I was in him. This lesson alone taught me that I cannot only rely on myself to make my life better but I cannot rely on the words of this world to define who I am either. What the world says about me are just like the trends of social media, one week its "poppin" and the next week "it's lit". It is forever misleading and changing. However, I desired more understanding of God and what he called me to do and in this I found myself being less concerned with the world and more focused on God. The names God called me are profound and unchanging.

I am more than a conqueror. I asked God, "why? Why did I have to go through all of that drama and hurt growing up?" What's interesting is that I received my answer and confirmation through a song I played all the time, but this time I knew it was confirmation because out of all the dozens of times I played this song, I actually heard his voice speak through it, "So when you try hurting me and even deserting me, know that I was designed to overcome adversity." Chile, I almost shouted. I had to stop the song and replay to make sure I was not hearing things, but he said it right the first time. I was looking around at my other coworkers just going about their daily work tasks and I am excited and about ready to shout like "you didn't hear that?!" God just said that I was DESIGNED to overcome adversity.

    I still smile in amazement about how great God is. In this same moment, God warned me to be humble about the understanding he is so willingly giving me because I could become oblivious to the judgment I place on someone for going through what he just delivered me from. Of course at times I had to ask for forgiveness for a little pettiness that ran through my mind, but, "We demolish arguments and every pretension that sets itself up against the knowledge of God, and we take captive every thought to make it obedient to Christ." In this, I learned not only to take captive of negative words that try to discount me from who God called me to be, but it teaches me to refuse the lies, disregard the disrespect, ignore the ignorance, of every negative speaking person that tries to convince me otherwise. Now, who I am in this day and age; I refuse to believe or even waste time on anything or anyone that is not helping me grow in every way. I have learned that the value of my peace of mind and worth is so precious and important that my entire energy will immediately have demons fleeing and avoiding trying me.

    If I say I am having a great day, it will be so, because my Father teaches and proves to me that "The tongue has the power of life and death, and those who love it will eat its fruit." (Proverbs 18:21) Therefore, I stand firm and even correct myself when I begin to pick up rotten fruit, (negative ways, words, thoughts, etc....) Because now that I know my worth and now that I know that I am more than what they said about me, I smile.

    Not because they tremble about me knowing their lies and manipulation has been exposed, but because I realize that every single word they spoke against me and thought negatively about me was actually who they really were and how they truly felt about themselves. It's always interesting to see people become exactly what they judged you for; but I am thankful for the adversity, because had I not gone through it, I would have never known how to kill the broken mentality that was placed over me. God is so intentional that I realized all this time, I was never fighting alone, and that I was actually walking in my purpose my entire life. Those moments of pain, abuse, and grief were only reminders that I am heading in the right direction but I need the one who can make the impossible, possible. God had my back and had the love I have longed for my entire life. Now, who I am today, well let me just humbly say, who I used to be wouldn't dare try me either.

A Bonus Just for you

Devoted To a Name

Finally it hit me. What you may ask? The truth about being devoted. The truth about my name. As a little girl I remember walking into an old church in Alabama. Wood floors and no air but some good church sanging. Watching my grandfather praise God. My 5 foot nothing grandad who could walk in the room and you can see the God in him. To go back to his roots where it all started. Red dirt, one gas station, and family love.
Good ol Alabama nothing but great memories. My granny on my mom side would be the first place I would visit.
Pink house and fly furniture plus home cooking. Those grits granny made I still until this day I cannot find any like that. To dream about speaking to my grandparents now would be amazing.
What hurts more is that each of them were the glue to our family. My grandfather is from my dad's side. I never meet my grandmother but I know her. From the stories from my dad, aunts, and uncles. My granny was not to be played with. A mother of 10 kids and a true women of God. My granny would be so proud of her grand girl. How
do I know because I am a lot like her. I have come to my embrace all of that.
My grandmother who is from my mom's side what a women of love. Not a dull moment with grandmother. A matter of fact nothing but laughs and hugs. How I miss her dearly. My mom's dad I never meet he passed well before my time. But like my granny Foster I know him too. Stories, pictures, and more stories lead me to where I am today.
My grandpa Ruffin was a business owner just like me. Now I see the mixture of all of my grandparents in one. Yes I am them!
Now they have all passed on and it hurts like hell. I've watched both sides of my family crumble. We were so broken. So broken

that we did not look at ourselves the same. We were just going through the motions.

The monarchs are gone so now what. Nothing that's what. Yep I said it and ain't ashamed to say it again. What happened to those weekends in Illinois? What happened to coming to Wisconsin just to hang? What happened to family is family and we love each other no matter what?
Where those just words or lies? I have yet to hear the answer but man those years after my grandpa passed just did not sit well with me at all. Who am I? A kid that is to be seen and not heard. I only did what I was told. Deep down I was hurting. I missed my cousins, aunts and uncles.

I remember my grandpa telling us and showing us the importance of family. How God designed the family and to stick together like glue. Do not allow the devil to come in and break anything up. What happened to that?
My grandmother preached and showed the same thing. But what happens when the glue passes on? Who will be the glue now? Are we so consumed in our pain that none of us can be the glue? Hold on to God's unchanging hand they say. Stay prayed up they say. Look to the hills they say. Death is apart of life they say. What about the kids that have been hurt by the division. The same kids that were told to be seen and not heard. We hurt too.

I've had sleepless nights and tears. To only dream of our family being put back together again. But no the adults just going on like they ain't hurting either.
What happened years later. We started to come together and not as often as we liked but we did. Even tho it felt different I knew it was needed.
To hear the laughter after telling stories about my grandpa. Music to my ears. My sister loved every bit of it. Let's just say our 6am talks were not boring or in vain. I remember my sister and I had been at my uncle's house in Illinois for my cousins graduation. All of us (cousins) got together and just talked about college and life. Nothing but laughs and genuine smiles. Me and my sister talk about that for a whole week.

After that everything just hit our family like a ton of bricks:
Cancer
Murder
Daily life struggles
Divorce Etc.
We were hit so hard we couldn't pick each other up because we were no longer superglued we were just tapped together.

Before 2010 I seen it but when my sister passed I felt it. Where are ya'll at? Where are my strongholds? Whose shoulder can I cry on?
I know call me if you need me they say.
I know I am here if you need anything they say. I know we are family they say.
Truth be told we are just tapped together.
Imagine going through a loss alone. Plus no support from either side of your family accept from one cousin.
Your best friend/cousin/sister. The one who you named the Godmother to your only daughter. The one who kept your best secrets. The one who called you in her time of need. All you could see was happiness and joy despite of everything. How many of us have this one cousin they love so much? You imagine yourself growing old with them. Raising your children together. Taking those memorable trips.
Shortly after my sister passed away. I encountered a situation that could leave me as the outcast of my family. Yes I have always been the outcast and I have always known this. I rarely said anything because I was devoted to the name. Devoted to the walk, devoted to the talk, and devoted to the untruth. Outcast, misfit, and misunderstood yep that's me!

While losing my sister I also lost my parents. Their grief and pain became mine which I did not get to deal at all. One day when I realized that my mom and I were shunned out I called my best cousin to vent. Why call her? I was so devoted to the family name that why not call my 1st cousin to vent. Besides we can't look bad to outsiders anyway.
As I was venting with pain and anger. My cousin stopped me in mid-sentence and said "Drea I don't want to get involved."

I felt so hurt. The hurt from the one person you thought was on your side. The one person that you held as they hurt. The one person that did not treat you like an outcast. Now to be outcasted by them! Let's be real I called to vent not for her opinion. A matter of fact she couldn't give me shit because her sister is a phone call away. Because I
bought the whole family dynamics I kept the situation in the family. Now what? I am completely alone. Just me being the stronghold for my parents and that's it.
Sometimes we crave something that isn't there. Like that candy bar that is at CVS but you at home. We crave it because we feel we want it. Question is do we need it?

To identify that while grieving is the hardest thing to do. It took me months to delete my cousins number. She didn't even call to check on me and no explanation at all. Just like that we were done.
I was already angry at God for taking my sister, pissed off at the devil because I am watching my parents mourn, and mad at myself because I thought family meant something. Just throw the whole situation away seriously.
I stopped writing.
I stopped being active in the community. It was hard for me to talk to anyone.
I lost myself. I mourned my cousin who lived on the other side of town. I missed our talks. I missed us going out for a drink. I lost my cousin as well as my sister in 2010. How do I come out of this? A question I had to stop asking myself because it was consuming me.
As I put it in my back pocket what I did not know is that it was hindering me emotionally and spiritually. From people being close to their sisters and cousins I grew bitter. Bitter with God mostly as well as others that were so happy about their family. Meanwhile my family celebrated a wedding without me, had family gatherings without me, and even graduation celebrations without me only showed me that I have to embrace me.
How do I do that and I am literally on an island by myself?

I had to give myself permission to feel. For so long I embodied everyone else's feelings. When it came time for me to feel I would instantly think about how my mom felt or how my husband was today. When I gave myself the okay to feel. I mean really feel the weight of pain started to lift off of me. The anger that held me hostage can't even hold a conversation with me anymore.

I had to forgive myself for dying inside. When you lose something or someone apart of you goes with them. It hurts like a papercut with rubbing alcohol on top. The depth of that is unexplainable. Daily as I mourned my cousin's friendship and watching her blossom standing on the sideline. I felt she did not feel anything when she left me hanging. I allowed that to fester for years. I was so worried about getting back at her and forgiving her that I did not forgive myself. Forgive myself for allowing this whole situation to consume me. By doing that I couldn't mourn the loss of my sister. I started to journal my thoughts and write down my pain. Not just by pin and paper but using a voice recorder. I could listen to it later and hear my pain.

I wrote down the lessons learned and counted the blessing earned. In the midst of all this my blessings out weighted the pain.
As I started my 60 day journey doing this I felt a relief and release come off of me. Then I could say with all confidence "Andrea I forgive you for allowing your pain to cloud your vision. I forgive you for allowing your hate to be a black dot over your love. I forgive you for allowing your smile to be fake. I love you with all of me." The start of healing is nothing easy. A matter of fact it ain't nothing to play with. Since I have been told to honor my name, honor my family, family is family, and to put God first. Is it Godly to leave your family hanging at the time of need? Is it Godly to walk away from everything you knew?
It's not and God has nothing to do with that. A matter of fact it's our pain that clouds us. Let's be serious here my anger with God through this whole ordeal was real. Why be angry at God when I allowed myself to believe what I've been told. Being devoted to a name. Being devoted to the myth.

At one point family meant something. What happened to that? Society hit, our flesh talking, and we so scared to get involved we hurt the ones that need us.
"Hurt people hurt people." How true us that!
As I started to really dissect my grief with losing my cousin. I learned that she was hurting too and didn't know how to be there for me. I had to accept and appreciate that.
Why do I appreciate that? Because her no meant a whole lot of work for me.
Rebooting my mindset and realizing that I am the
queen of my queendom. Understanding that everyone is not for you. No shade just truth.
Believing in the alignment of who you are and your journey will lead you to the key people you will need in your life. DNA related or not.
It took years to get here and when I seen my cousin for the first time in 2016 all I could do was hug her. We've released what we needed to. No apology but more love. When I started to realize the apology I wanted wasn't meant for me to get. I accepted that my soul, mind, and spirit didn't need it. What I needed was love. Even if it took years I knew I had to wait for God's timing.

"In the midst of the storm know that what it seems like it ain't like. We miss the light by seeing the dark." Andrea A. Moore

ABOUT THE AUTHORS

Sherri Leopold
Sherri Strohecker Leopold has worked in the Network Marketing/Direct Selling industry for 20 years, gaining experience in speaking, mentoring and team building. She is an Independent Brand Promoter for Le-Vel, a leader in health and wellness industry and currently lives in Springfield IL. As a veteran in this industry, she remains passionate about encouraging others to create their destiny. She loves helping others develop both physical and financial success. She coaches and mentors a large team all over the world. She is also the Editor for the Healthy Lifestyles column for Exposure Magazine. Outside of business, she is happily married to Scott Leopold for over 30 years. Together, they have three grown children. She is also a fur mom to six felines and has spent many years helping the feline rescue, Forever Home Feline Ranch. Sherri enjoys writing, reading, painting and drawing in her free time.

Artist bio: Hope Marshall is a native of the DC Metro area. An only child, and insistent on doing things backward, she served 7 years in the U.S. Navy, and then, went to college. She later graduated from Towson University with a BS in Sociology/Anthropology. Additionally, she served as an AmeriCorps VISTA. By day, Hope works as an instructor, and freelance proofreader and editor. Hope's writing/performing repertoire include: Stoop Stories' "Unquiet Minds", Stevenson University's Quad Stories' "Fail Better: The Upside to Falling Down", and Washington Improv Theatre's Student Showcase. Nights, pre-dawn hours, and weekends find her tinkering around with *@cornygirlchronicles*, a creative outlet of apparel, stationery, and overall, the persnickety ramblings of the overly insightful. Hope is the daughter of Caribbean immigrants, an avid reader, and a cat lover. This anthology will be her first, formal authorship.

Kyla D. Lurry is the CEO and founder of KylaNicole, LLC, an international speaker, author, and an expert in laws and public policy analysis. Kyla developed a passion for empowerment at an early age, dedicating her time and works to inspire, coach and invest in the minds and hearts of both men and women though the KylaNicole Brand. Kyla specializes in overcoming Trauma and building businesses from a legal aspect.

In stimulating development, self-awareness, and true authenticity, Kyla has accomplished her goals by engaging in and hosting a series of events including "Loud Discussions" panels which feature open discussions of a variety of life themes, helpful tools and concepts from her self-help book titled "15 Ways To Improve Your Reality, radio, magazine and her multiple eBooks, including "Why you're broke, A Broken Egg, and The Art of Self-Love". She is active in her community as a youth leader and is devoted to philanthropy! Kyla has extensive training and an advanced background in laws, policies, and stipulations that will impact your brand.

Kyla has attained her Doctorate from Walden University in Law and Public Policy Administration, successfully completed coursework at Florida Coastal Law School, her Master's of Science in Corporate Organizational Communication from Northeastern University as well as her life coach certification. For more information and insight on the services offered by KylaNicole, please check out her website www.KylaNicole.Org.

D'Neshia Johnson-Shields is a 26 year old young and a newlywed who married her high school crush (lol). She is optimistic, hardworking, and loves laughing. As she started growing writing became her first language and then speaking is my second. It helped her express pain and truth. She is currently in school studying human services while working a full-time job. She maintains a pretty low profile when it comes to social interaction, however given the opportunity she is a force to be reckoned with.

Life has not always been easy for Mrs. Shields. Throughout life she faced adversity from various sorts of attacks but with the the grace and strength of God she overcame them all. Her testimony is the epitome from grief to grind:I gained strength, courage, and wisdom. I am beyond grateful because at a time what I thought would end my life resulted in the birth of it. I have been walking in fear of my truth majority of my life but now given this opportunity, I hope to give someone the courage to tell theirs.

Myesha Monique Collins is a native of Los Angeles, California, raised in Pomona, CA., currently residing in Chesapeake, VA with her three sons. Myesha is
an Ordained Minister, Service Connected Disabled Veteran, Author, Speaker, Creative Strategist and Motivational Experience Coach. Myesha has a background in Administration, Sociology, Human Resources, Quality Assurance, Continuous Quality Improvement, Management, Leadership, and Training.
Myesha's Monique Collins first book was a book of poetry and short stories, entitled *Poetration*, was self-published in 2006 and is available through Amazon. In 2017, Myesha spearheaded an anthology, *Blue Girl Turned Gold*, inspired by Myesha's non-profit organization, Blue Girls Turned Gold. Blue Girls Turned Gold is a national organization whose mission is to empower women. Blue Girls Turned Gold currently host 6 Creative valuable workshops to empower!
Myesha prides herself on her ability to use her intuition and experience to find creative strategies to turn women from BLUE

(not knowing how great they are) to GOLD (knowing how great they are). Myesha has been interviewed by Exposure Magazine, Indiana Tuggle, and Goodwill Good works to discuss her current and future works and projects. Myesha has 2 additional therapeutic works being published this year, Reclaiming My Time from the 9-5 Grind set to be released May 2018 and From Grief to Grind ignited by Andrea A. Moore set to be released August 2018.

Myesha recently joined the "Genius is Common Movement," founded by Bruce George, visionary creator of Def Poetry Jam after seeing how much the movement was in alignment with her purpose and mission. She lives the Genius is Common movement daily using her creativity and pushing those to see the GENIUS within.

Myesha has a connection to intuition and spirituality and loves helping people see their greatness within. Her non profit Blue Girls Turned Gold has the specific mission of women empowerment. She is a firm believer that people of all ages need help, and enjoys passing on her own experiences and knowledge that will help with whatever they are going through, and come out of it stronger than ever. She is a firm believer that 'Experience shape who you are, but they do not dictate who you become".

You can contact Myesha Monique Collins at bluegirlsturnedgold@gmail.com- Email
www.bluegirlsturnedgold.org - Web
Etsy.com/shop/bluegirlsturnedgold- Etsy #Blue Girls Turned Gold- Instagram @BlueTurnedGold- Twitter 770-988-4089- Phone

Phoenix J Ma'ri moved to Harker Heights, Texas from Cameron, NC after making a decision to leave a reproachful husband in 2012. She studied psychology and sociology at Fayetteville State University and Texas A&M University Central Texas. Although she has not graduated, her desire to finish her learning will soon be in Integrated Psychology. Passionate about empowering women, especially military spouses the move back to Central Texas was truly aligned by God. In 2015, Voice II Voices, an empowering outreach for healing women was birthed through the ending pain of a 20 year marriage where she felt betrayed, and due to all those years of unemployment, the voice which was taken became her rising force.

Phoenix J Ma'ri is determined to help others after she survived a nervous breakdown in March 2017 due to her divorce and unbearable grief of herself. She entered the hospital as an untreated bipolar, depressed, suicidal black woman, but came out on a healing journey with fire blazing. She searched for years to find help in her healing, only to learn it was within her. She has engulfed her path with flames of passion to assist women to rise victoriously by resetting the mind, body, and soul, especially after a traumatic event.

This rebirth God took Phoenix though helped to rebirth her God-given identity through spiritual awakening, awareness, and healing. She is a Reiki Practitioner, Intuitive Reader, and Chakra Energy Healer, a co-host on The Real Housewives, and the co-host of The Tee's Corner Wake Up Show via podcast. She is a member of Black Women in Business where she serves on the Executive Team Member Committee and the Committee Lead for the Mentoring Program, Mentors Matters, and she is also a member of Black CEOs Central Texas.

Phoenix J Ma'ri is passionate about empowering women, especially military spouses the move back to Central Texas was truly aligned by God. In 2015, Voice II Voices, an empowering outreach for healing women was birthed through the ending pain of a 20 year marriage where she felt betrayed, and due to all those years of unemployment, the voice which was taken became her rising force.

Dorsetta Denise (Clark) Davis was born May 26, 1966 to Betty A. Clark and Thomas L. Smith. She has 1 sister (Darilyn) and 1 brother (Thomas).

Dorsetta joined the army right after graduating high school in 1984. Her duty assignments included Fort Ord, California; Stuttgart, Germany; Fort Leonard Wood, Missouri; Friedberg, Germany; Yong San, Korea; and Fort Sill, Oklahoma. While stationed in Friedberg, Germany, Dorsetta was deployed to South West Asia in support of Operation Desert Shield/Desert Storm. Her awards include 5 Army Accommodation Medals, Army Achievement Medal, 3 Overseas Medals, Southwest Asia Medal and many other achievements and accolades. Dorsetta received an Associates Degree in Business and a Bachelors Degree in Criminal Justice from Cameron University in Oklahoma. She also earned a Dual Masters Degree in Business Administration and Health Care Administration from Trident University in California.

Dorsetta married in 1988 and divorced in 2000. She has 4 children John (passed in 2010), Ronnell, Jeremiah and Jasmine (adopted out at birth).

After retiring from the army in 2005, after 21+ years, she worked several different jobs as a college library secretary; disabled veteran service officer, medical services clerk, administrative assistant and a healthcare specialist before medically retiring in 2016. Dorsetta started her own business as a credit repair specialist in 2013 and with many name changes, finally formed Joyful Wealth Solutions, where wealth is rooted in wisdom and manifested in joy, with her business partner, Nicole in January 2018. As the owner and certified debt specialist, she has been able to establish systems that has helped many individuals and families with financial freedom. She is also a member of the Business Networking International (BNI), Black Women in Business (BWIB) and Chief Operating Officer of The New Twenty-Four, a suicide awareness site dedicated to the memory of her late son John Curtis IV.

Dorsetta strives everyday to leave a legacy for her 4 grandchildren, Davion, Ke`Mya, Ra`Nyah and John.

Dorsetta Denise (Clark) Davis married in 1988 and divorced in 2000. She has 4 children John (passed in 2010), Ronnell, Jeremiah and Jasmine (adopted out at birth).

After retiring from the army in 2005, after 21+ years, she worked several different jobs as a college library secretary; disabled veteran service officer, medical services clerk, administrative assistant and a healthcare specialist before medically retiring in 2016. Dorsetta started her own business as a credit repair specialist in 2013 and with many name changes, finally formed Joyful Wealth Solutions, where wealth is rooted in wisdom and manifested in joy, with her business partner, Nicole in January 2018. As the owner and certified debt specialist, she has been able to establish systems that has helped many individuals and families with financial freedom. She is also a member of the Business Networking International (BNI), Black Women in Business (BWIB) and Chief Operating Officer of The New Twenty-Four, a suicide awareness site dedicated to the memory of her late son John Curtis IV.

Nicole "Coach Red" Redmond is her own boss of Redmond Legacy Coaching, LLC. Her mantra is, "Leave behind a legacy, not a liability", a holistic expression. She is also the co-owner of Joyful Wealth Solutions and co-founder of M.A.D. About Your Business Organization. Some may know her as poet, NicciFaye, who is intentional on stimulating the human conscious through her spoken word stories. She is a mental health advocate, domestic abuse survivor, and wealth and financial facilitator. She is also a Veteran of the U.S. Army, mother to a teen solopreneur, and devoted wife.

Her purposes are founded on a God-given revelation of three pillars; Spiritual, Mental, and Financial. She serves these purposes through the capacity of coaching, consulting, workshops, webinars, writing, community work, and spoken word.

She is author of *Walk In My Words, or Ride In My Back Pocket*, a book of poetic collections, co-author in *The Money Code and How to Crack It*, and *From Grief to Grind: The Journey of Denial, Acceptance, and Purpose*. She is working on upcoming book ventures. She is Brooklyn born, raised in Tampa, Florida,

and resides in Central Texas. She has Master's Degree in Psychology. One of her goals is to be a licensed Mental Health and Chemical Dependency Counselor in the state of Texas.
"Nothing will work, unless you do" ~Maya Angelou~
Her contact information
Brands: Nicole Redmond, Coach Red, NicciFaye
Social Media:
https://www.facebook.com/RedmondLegacyCoaching/
https://www.facebook.com/M.A.D.BIZWOMEN/
Business Email:
Redmond Legacy Coaching:
RedmondLegacyCoaching@gmail.com **Joyful Wealth Solutions:** joyfulwealthsolutions@gmail.com
M.A.D. About Your Business madbizwomen@gmail.com
NicciFaye: niccifaye1spoken4@gmail.com

www.ingramcontent.com/pod-product-compliance
Lightning Source LLC
Chambersburg PA
CBHW021956090426
42811CB00001B/47